D1510092

Think Yourself to the Riches of Life

ROBERT CONKLIN

CB

CONTEMPORARY
BOOKS

CHICAGO

Library of Congress Cataloging-in-Publication Data

Conklin, Robert.
    Think yourself to the riches of life / Robert Conklin.
        p.   cm.
    ISBN 0-8092-3889-6 (cloth)
        1. Success—Psychological aspects.   I. Title.
    BF637.S8C644   1992
    158'.1—dc20   92-5517
                                                              CIP

Published by Contemporary Books, Inc.
180 North Michigan Avenue, Chicago, Illinois 60601
Manufactured in the United States of America
International Standard Book Number: 0-8092-3889-6

Also by Robert Conklin:

The Dynamics of Positive Attitudes
Ego-Bionics
The Power of a Magnetic Personality
Positive Mind Album
Adventures in Attitudes
LifePower
Reach for the Sun
How to Get People to Do Things

Contents

Acknowledgments

I am grateful to the Carlson Learning Co. for permission to use limited excerpts from *Adventures in Attitudes, Life-Power*, and the *Positive Mind Album* in this book. Further information about these programs may be obtained from:

Carlson Learning Company
Carlson Parkway
P.O. Box 59159
Minneapolis, MN 55459-8247
(612) 449-2824

I also deeply appreciate the guidance and support of my friend Sakan Yanagidaira, 2-10-25 Mita, Meguro-Ku, Tokyo, Japan, who translated and is responsible for introducing my books and programs to more than half a million of the Japanese people.

Prologue

Look for the Ponies

It was Christmas morning.

In the rich family's big house the little boy began opening his presents.

Alas! Nothing was quite right. The sled was too small, and the toy train did not have enough cars; the games were the wrong kind, and so on. Nothing seemed to suit him.

Out in the back the stable boy woke in the hayloft and looked around, hoping to see a toy or two. Seeing nothing, he scrambled down the ladder to the stables below.

The only things in sight down there were piles of manure.

Gleefully the boy clapped his hands and cried, "Wow! There has to be a pony here someplace!"

Therein rests the joy and wisdom of life: look for the ponies!

Will Rogers, America's homespun philosopher, once said, "Life is 10 percent what you make it and 90 percent how you take it."

There is always a pony behind life's problems! Learning to look for the ponies brings richness and meaning to your life!

You become empowered by your adversities, obstacles,

and despair! Experiencing problems always gives you an opportunity to grow and move ahead.

Your darkest moment can disappear if you learn to find rays of light! No matter how hopeless a situation may seem, it is only an illusion waiting to be transformed into an advantage.

You can change any condition in your life by looking for the pony. Change your thoughts, your attitude, and the situation will change.

That is simply a recognition of one of life's oldest truths: life is an extension of thought.

Your life is what your thoughts make it. More than four thousand years ago, it was written, "As one's thinking is, such one becomes."

What you are depends on the thoughts you hold in your mind. Change your thoughts, and you will change your life!

The process sounds simple. Choose your thoughts and you are choosing the pattern of your life. Actually, however, it is quite profound. For thoughts are like feathers blown about in the wind.

Thoughts whirl about in the mind as reactions to everyday encounters. Try as best one can, thoughts at times run out of control, creating anger, resentment, envy, discouragement, and a variety of other unwanted feelings.

The purpose of this book is to help you take charge of your thoughts and feelings. You have the power to choose your thoughts. This book will help you define and use that power to live life more abundantly and joyfully.

The book will deal with a series of everyday episodes and problems that you face. It will help you find the pony, the opportunity, behind every problem and life's daily experiences.

1

The Miracle of Your Mind

Life is an extension of thought. Master the mansions of your mind, and you have gained dominion over your life.

Within you is your mind—an intricate computer that stores the thoughts that you choose day by day. These are molds that program and shape your life. Sages of all times have realized this. Marcus Aurelius wrote, "Look well into thyself; there is a source which will always spring up if thou wilt always search there."

The fate and fortune of your life are resting, right now, in the hidden chambers of your mind—your mind, the most magnificent and awesome creation of the universe. The incredible strength and energy the mind is capable of producing in the body are almost unbelievable.

A frightened five-foot farm wife, for example, lifted a two-thousand-pound tractor to free her husband, who was pinned underneath. Later it took three husky men to right the tractor.

A twelve-year-old boy lifted a fallen log from the legs of his father. Four men could barely move it later on.

In Scotland a great eagle swooped down and carried an infant to its nest on a cliff. The strongest climbers in the village attempted to scale the steep wall but had to turn back.

Then the slightly built mother, whose only experience in climbing had been the stairs of her simple cottage, started up the steep incline. She made it to the top as villagers looked on in fear-stricken awe, took the baby from the nest, and then, even more miraculously, descended with the baby in her arms.

There are many similar cases on record in which feats of almost unbelievable strength have been accomplished.

What happens in these situations? The body does not suddenly become bigger or the muscles any larger; no new skills are learned. The only change in the body is what is produced by a change in the mind.

The mind suddenly has a goal it knows must be achieved. It is not burdened and limited by doubt, disbelief, or cynicism. So it soars to its magnificent levels of accomplishment, unrestrained by the human chains of thought.

Other Amazing Powers

But the mind has other capabilities perhaps even more significant. Scientists now believe that the mind may be almost like a television set in its ability to receive certain images and sensations when "tuned in" to events many miles away.

For example, a woman awoke suddenly at 2:30 in the morning seeing the terror-stricken face of her son. She lay awake the rest of the night, unable to remove the vision from her mind.

At 7:00 A.M., she received a phone call from three hundred miles away informing her that her son had survived a nearly fatal car accident at 2:30 that morning.

The memory power of the mind is infinite. It can hold more facts than are contained in the millions of books in the Smithsonian Institution. Evidence now indicates that the memory of the mind is almost perfect.

During a brain operation on a young man, the surgeon's instrument happened to touch a nerve of the youth. Spontaneously he began to mumble. By coincidence a tape recorder was being used, and the words that flowed from the young man's mouth were recorded. When the conversation was played to the mother, she was amazed to discover that the things he described had actually happened when he was six months old.

This amazing ability to memorize and recall is within every individual but is seldom recognized, due to its lack of use, and is inhibited by the conviction that "we have a poor memory."

The mind is the control center of your body. It makes thousands of decisions every day, regulating and maintaining your physical condition. Thoughts and emotions influence these decisions. Unhealthy thoughts are translated into an unhealthy body.

Scientists tell us that there are mind-controlled mechanisms to resist sickness. When the mind is preserving positive, wholesome thoughts, these mechanisms work effectively. When the mind, however, becomes swamped with negative thoughts such as despondency, anxiety, or hate, the mechanisms break down and one becomes sick.

For years doctors have used the attitudes of the mind to heal their patients. They have been using the most miraculous of the wonder drugs to do so. This wonder drug is a pill called the *placebo*. It is a nothing pill. It can be a bright-colored capsule or a sugar-coated pill. It holds a harmless powder.

But when doctors prescribe it with authority and confidence, it often produces remarkable recoveries for their patients. It sometimes even causes the "side effects" of the strong drugs.

It is effective because it changes the patient's thinking. And when the thinking is changed, the condition of the body is changed.

Little wonder that sages throughout the ages have observed that life is, in reality, an extension of thought.

Life Reflects Thoughts

Cicero proclaimed, "To think is to live." All of your living is actually done in your thinking! Your experiences, your successes, and, yes, even your failures occur first and last in your thinking.

The frustration of life is that the principles of thought, the development of successful ways of thinking, remain hidden. You must discover them for yourself. They are not found in the schools or your normal learning experiences.

Of this you can be certain, however: good thoughts and actions bring good results; bad thoughts and actions create bad results.

The Greatest Gift of Life

In describing what was wrong with people of his day, Albert Schweitzer, Nobel Prize winner, said, "They simply do not think." He realized that people are "thinking" every waking moment—but not to the depths of their abilities. They are not managing their minds—choosing the thoughts that are going to guide them directly to their goals, dreams, and hopes. They are not using their great gift of choosing their thoughts. They are merely reacting, often negatively. And when those negative thoughts start piling up, that's what their lives become—a negative experience.

Have you ever thought that you had too much on your mind? Perhaps you felt that you were caught in a massive net of care, responsibility, drudgery, discouragement, or burden. You had the feeling that you were weighed down with worry about, concern over, and fear of the things that would or wouldn't happen to you in the future.

This dull, dragging mood presses on you, sapping your energy and shutting out your zest for everyday activity. You find yourself saying "I just can't seem to get going. I've got too many things on my mind."

How many things can you have on your mind at any one time?

Only one of course. It's impossible to think of more than one "thing" at a time! You might feel that you have too much on your mind because this one thought on your mind is negative. It might be a thought of anxiety, concern, resentment, dejection, pessimism, hopelessness, or lack of confidence in yourself. Any one of those shaggy, stagnating thoughts can create the feeling of burden, of an immense weight on the mind.

However, the realization that you can have only one thing on your mind at a time will lead you to an awareness of one of your greatest gifts! It is this: *you are given the ability to choose that one thought on your mind!*

The human being alone, of all life, is given the gift of choice of thought. A frog cannot choose its thoughts. All it knows how to do is react. A dog has neither the will nor the power to choose thoughts. A dog knows how to be only a dog. This gift is your most cherished heritage. It is worth more to you than all of your talents, your physical attributes, or the riches and pleasures of the world. You do not fully appreciate this gift until you are deprived of it.

The newspapers told of a man who walked into a police station to confess a crime he had committed fifteen years before. The reason for his confession? "I have not been able to get it off my mind."

In other words, he had been deprived of his ability to choose the one thought on his mind! The one thought that kept appearing was the crime he had committed and the guilt it created! He was willing to subject himself to punishment—welcomed it in fact—in return for the restoration of his birthright, the ability to choose the one thought on his mind.

Your Ultimate Freedom

In an inspiring book entitled *Man's Search for Meaning*, psychologist Viktor Frankl described his experiences in a

German concentration camp during World War II. While there, he was subjected to all sorts of brutal and inhuman treatment. But he lived, while most died. He lived because he wanted to live. Others lost their will to live because their minds became consumed by the tormenting misery of their existence. He, on the other hand, singled out any small incident of positive meaning and let his mind dwell on that. An extra crust of bread or a shoelace would bring joy and significance to his day. His frightful experience in captivity revealed to him that electric fences, chains, locks, and cells do not deprive an individual of freedom.

"One's ultimate freedom is the ability to choose one's attitude in any given set of circumstances," he discovered.

Not until you have learned to use your ability to choose your own attitudes have you achieved the freedom to be your own person, reaching out for any goal or dream of your choice. Without this freedom you are the captive of every habit, situation, circumstance, or surrounding in which you find yourself.

What an incredible gift, then, this is—the ability to choose the thoughts that dwell within your mind! You can choose your thoughts and, by so doing, choose the pathways of your life. For your life is merely a reflection of your thoughts.

What do you want out of life? More money? More happiness? More friends? More success in business? You have no further to look than within yourself!

2

Manage Your Thoughts

Your state of consciousness today will be your state of being in the future. Understand that statement and you will be able to predict your unborn tomorrows. Comprehend the impact of those words and you can create and control your destiny. Without that awareness your life can be a helter-skelter journey of aimless frustration.

Your state of consciousness today will be your state of being in the future. Come along as we study the significance of that principle around which your life is centered.

Your state of consciousness refers to the thoughts, images, and attitudes you hold in your mind. A thought held in the mind for a period of time becomes an attitude and then is infallibly impressed into your life. The attitude becomes the blueprint for tomorrow's experience.

Remember that an idea or thought always precedes the experience. Look about you at all that has been created by human effort—buildings, cars, roads, bridges, and gardens. They all began as an idea in someone's mind.

So it is with your life. Your thoughts of today will be your experiences of the future. That is true whether those thoughts are created deliberately by you, with joy and harmony, or run harum-scarum from ear to ear as your reaction to a befuddled world. You have the power to control your life! You, like all human beings, have choices.

You are empowered by your imagination. With your imagination you can construct the visions, the pictures, of what you want your life to be. Whatever those visions are, they will be realized in some fashion in the future.

Your state of consciousness today will be your state of being in the future.

What you hold in your mind today will shape your experiences of tomorrow. That is the one profound thread of wisdom common to the civilizations of all ages. Each philosopher expresses it a bit differently, but it boils down to the same meaning. Life, as the human being experiences it, is an extension of thought.

How could such a simple idea be so misunderstood and misused? Few people actually comprehend and direct the cause-and-effect thought forces that exist within them.

Many people, believing they're on the right rails, get detoured into doubt and discouragement.

Principle of Thought

A study of the principles of thought might explain why. Let's look at that first sentence again: your state of consciousness today will be your state of being tomorrow.

You might say, "I've been doing that. I want to get ahead. I've been trying to lose weight, give up smoking, treat the kids better, get rid of my ulcers and headaches, and nothing much is happening. It doesn't work for me."

Doesn't it? Let's take a closer look. Sparked by ambition, one person thinks, "I'm going to work harder, overcome my laziness, learn more, and try saving money." That's the state of consciousness. What will be the state of being tomorrow? Simple—working harder, overcoming laziness, learning more, and trying to save money.

Another says, "For years I've tried everything to lose weight. I've gone to Super-Skinny, Pound-Pushers, Weight-Wizards, made bets with friends, been scared sleepless by my doctor, and my weight still is like a yo-yo. Goes up and down." That's a statement of consciousness, isn't it? What will be the state of being tomorrow? The same as it has been for all those yesterdays: struggling with weight, food, and calories—sometimes winning, sometimes losing.

Learn to Visualize

To manage the energy of thought to greater advantage is to bring into use the human being's unique gift—the visual imagination. It is quite possibly the least used of all the human talents, except by those who instinctively require its use in their daily work. The artist visualizes the picture before it goes on canvas. The pilot sees the landing in all its dimensions before the wheels touch the ground. The professional golfer pictures the swing and the shot before striking the ball.

The lesson is clear. Hold in your consciousness exactly what it is you want to be instead of what you are. "That's not reality," you say. "It's just daydreaming. I'd be kidding myself." Would you? Human beings have the ability to envision who they would like to be and who they are capable of becoming. For many this lies dormant, never used. Why not use it to shape your existence and choose what you will become?

Fasten in your mind all the details of the success that you want. Know that you have already arrived. Give up the groping, hoping, someday wishes that perhaps it will happen to you.

Realize the love, depth, and richness of the relationships all about you. Envision yourself as a loved and loving person rather than lonely and bored, reaching out for someone who can make you happy.

Give up the self-concept of an overweight person jousting with extra pounds. Visualize that slender person within you waiting to emerge. Buy the clothing you will soon be wearing. Start being the person you want to be.

Stop believing that you're a fragile sack of flesh and

bones, defenseless against sickness and age. Health and vitality are the natural and ageless qualities of the human being. Don't think of yourself as a sick person trying to get better. Claim your perfection now, and that will be your state of being tomorrow.

Remember, your state of consciousness today will be your state of being tomorrow.

Use "I Am"

Realize the incredible significance of the two words *I am*! Whatever your hopes and dreams for the future, know that they are yours if you learn the power of "I am." Replace "I will," "I hope," "I would like," and all the other wistful wishes with "I am."

If it's success you want, know in your heart that you're already there. Picture all that success means to you—the home, security, financial independence, travel, and adventure. Pull it out of the musty dream stage and plant it firmly in your mind. Declare that you have that now. Use the words "I am!" That becomes your state of consciousness. It will, inevitably, become your state of being in the future.

You see, if you're hoping to be successful someday, plugging along day after day, longing for more of the good things in life, that is your state of consciousness. What, then, will be your state of being in the future? It will be hoping to be successful someday, plugging along day after day, longing for more of the good things in life.

Your state of conviction or consciousness today will be your state of being in the future. Life is meant to be lived with vigor, vitality, and good health. But only if you believe that is true. Let sickly negative thoughts creep into your mind, and they will surely shape your being in the future.

Indeed, it's not easy to declare your good health when your body is claiming illness. To say "I am complete, whole, healthy, and perfect" instead of thinking "I hope I get better" may seem hypocritical. But in a deeper sense it is quite the opposite. For one of the most potent forces of nature is the principle of healing and restoration. That perfect principle is within you and working for your good if you believe it.

Look Within Yourself

Have you ever wondered why some relationships bump along in a rocky fashion at times? Look no further than your own expectations and attitudes. You might think others are always to blame. They have treated you thoughtlessly or unjustly. That is your state of consciousness. The relationship won't be much different in the future unless you scour your mind of all negative thoughts about the people involved.

Thus you hear the advice to love unconditionally. You can never be completely happy or healthy unless you can forgive. Set aside the negative critical thoughts about others and love unconditionally. That is your state of consciousness. Your state of being will be one filled with love and harmony.

Examine all the corners of your life. How are your energy and enthusiasm? What are your work habits and productivity? Are you getting as big a slice of life as you would like to have?

If you're lacking in any of the riches of life, apply the "I am" strategy. Practiced consistently, it will lead to deep-seated belief, a state of consciousness.

3

Get Rid of Swampy

There is a scratchy little voice that sloshes around in one's noggin in whatever soggy bog it can create. Maybe it comes from some wizened troll called Swampy.

Swampy is a scrubby little gnome with a mouth that turns down even when he smiles. You can't look into his eyes, because they're covered by his eyebrows; his laugh gurgles out like a chorus of squeaky door hinges. Swampy has long arms floating, bending, and grasping like snaky spider webs. You never notice them until they've reached out and wrapped themselves around you and started pulling you toward his swamp. He wears lead boots up to his waist. When he clings to you, you feel as if you're dragging bags of cement.

Swampy will make sure you hold on to all your negative thoughts and behaviors. For example, when you criticize and blame others, Swampy will croak with delight. "Let 'em have it!" he'll say. "Get mad! Show 'em you can't be pushed around!"

Swampy will deceive you into believing he is your only friend. It's strange, though, how he can seem so right and yet make you feel so awful.

Listen to Swampy and you will never overexert yourself. He'll remind you, "Where is all that work going to get you? Ulcers? High blood pressure? Besides, look at the others who will benefit. That company, for example. What has it really done for you?"

Swampy has some shaggy advice about helping others. "Listen," he'll say. "People are using you. Casting your bread on the waters is a real bummer. It gets all soggy and sinks. Hang onto it. Watch out for yourself. No one else is going to do it."

About the future, Swampy predicts nothing but utter hopelessness. "Don't you read your newspapers and watch TV? There's nothing but sickness, violence, tragedy, and danger out there. Don't expect too much out of life and you'll never be disappointed. You're much better off right here in the swamp with me."

Believe that and Swampy will sell you some of his ground for nothing down and a few hours of dejection each week. You'll spend time there thinking that you're misunderstood, unappreciated, overworked, underpaid, and victimized by life's misfortunes.

Blame others for your companionship with Swampy and you will remain with him. Because Swampy does not come to you; you go to Swampy. By your own choice. Accept that fact. It will eventually free you from Swampy.

You Choose Your Thoughts

You are responsible for your thoughts. It isn't really Swampy who put that junk between your ears. Nor is it your mate, who forgot to tell you how lovable you are. Nor is it your cousin Albert, who still owes you $90 from four years ago. Nor is it that prospect who treated you like leftover lutefisk.

Nope. Those people didn't put those raspy thoughts up there. You did it. But you can remove what you put there. It isn't easy, but you can do it. With that realization comes the mastery of your life.

At some point in life almost everyone inevitably

reaches the conclusion that life is a reflection of thought. We can actually trace our experiences in life back to thoughts and recognize that thoughts constantly held in the mind become reality.

Wonderful! All we have to do to build a magnificent life is to build positive thoughts and actions, and they become reality. Is it that easy? Let's see how we construct our concepts of reality.

Our minds are like high-fidelity recorders. They record experiences, words, ideas, and events to which we are exposed. These are never erased. They play back in our minds and become reality. Accumulated in our minds are many negative recordings that are so deeply embedded we do not even recognize they exist.

You see, our lives as babies are our only thoroughly positive experiences. Then we are loved. Totally loved. When we begin to walk, a process that builds our negativism begins. To prepare us to fit into a complex and highly regimented society we are restrained, punished, criticized, restricted, and molded. We are not given a large portion of the love we once knew.

Negative Thoughts Acquired

The whole process cannot help building up resistance and resentment at the very least. In some instances these feelings break out into open hate and defiance.

We tend to suppress these feelings, think of ourselves as bad, and feel guilty.

In a society based on materialistic values we become economic beings. Success is making money; happiness and security become dollar-oriented. We are taught this at an early age. "Learning how to handle money" it is called. It becomes an integral part of the family relationship. We acquire a variety of feelings (many negative) about the way we spend money, whether we are children, husbands, or wives. A majority of divorces are rooted in financial stress.

So we find ourselves competing. Competing not only

for money, position, and power but also for recognition, acceptance, and love. In our society competition is encouraged. It becomes a virtue. So our relationships become contests. Someone wins, and someone loses. Or someone is charging us too much or paying us too little.

We are taught to beware of strangers. We lock ourselves inside our homes at night. As children we are told to strike back when struck. Our language is filled with *fight*— "fight for what is yours"; "fight for success." Our toys are guns and lethal devices; our games are "cops and robbers." Crime and violence become a source of sordid interest and pleasure. Our newspapers, movies, and TV shows are filled with it.

Our attitudes become antagonistic, suspicious, belligerent, sometimes angry and hateful toward others.

Our environment becomes our enemy. It is polluted. It is filled with smog, drafts, smoke, pollens, and humidity that we are told are harmful. We hate bugs, weeds, germs, and dirt. We sterilize, sanitize, and fill the air, our yards, and our homes with poisons.

In our search for comfort we find days too hot or too cold, too wet or too dry. So we must control the temperature to control our mood.

Our TVs and newspapers warn us about heart attacks, cancer, headaches, stomach gas, and a variety of other ills and dangers.

We are overwhelmed with information about the things that make us sick; little is said about the magnificent forces that keep us well. So we think more about sickness than about health. And—remember?—thoughts inevitably become reality. So, "That which you greatly fear has come upon you!"

We Hang On to Garbage

We, as human beings, enjoy the customs of eating. Formal processes might vary, but the procedures have little variance whether we're dining at home or in the cafeteria.

But alas! What we hold in esteem about feeding the body we woefully neglect in caring for the mind.

Most of us do not prepare our minds, as we would our bodies, for the days ahead. We do not put together fresh ingredients or use stimulating recipes.

The greatest tragedy, however, is that yesterday's garbage is tenaciously clutched and mixed in with today's mental menus. What we would find revolting in the preparation of food for the body we cling to in feeding the mind. So here is the mind, the control center of life, trying to reach out for happiness, purpose, and satisfaction, burdened with a lot of junk—months and years of accumulated garbage. Little wonder that people feel held back—hopeless and frustrated in careers and relationships.

It isn't that we don't want to dispose of all the clinkers in our thinkers. It is just that the garbage is so elusive—like watermelon seeds. We try to get ahold of those thoughts, and they squirt away, only to pop up another day in another experience. Where does the rubbish come from?

Swampy does a pretty good sell job convincing us it is reality, doesn't he?

What's the Solution?

Described here are only a few of the channels by which negative thoughts find their way into our heads and become so deep-seated they are almost completely hidden in our minds. You may or may not have experienced some or all of these thoughts.

Is there a way out? Of course. But it requires day-to-day mental effort. Look at the world as being friendly and magnificent. Enjoy the warmth of the sun, the chill of the winter wind. Walk in the rain, look up at the stars, watch a bird fly, smell the clover, stroke an animal, lie down in a meadow, and be awed by a setting sun. Stop being in conflict with your world, saying the day is too hot or too cold or hating the friendly dandelion or beetle in your front yard. Learn to live in harmony with your environment.

Love. *Really* love, that is. Know that you are one with everything and everyone. Love people. Stop competing; strive only for personal excellence. Stop judging others. Find others interesting even if they are different from you.

Look at every situation in life and say "There has to be a pony here someplace."

Within every human exists the true being, the same that rests within you—spiritual, perfect, unlimited.

Let your mind dwell on these things every moment, every day, and you will gradually become aware of and grow into a life of positive thinking and experience.

4

Think Big!

"The most significant mistake that I've made in my business career was that I didn't think big enough." Eyebrows went up on the faces of the luncheon group that day in Boise, Idaho. For it was a surprising statement by a man whose wealth has been estimated by *Forbes* to exceed $500 million!

Jack Simplot started in Idaho as a potato picker. He eventually became the world's largest processor of potatoes. His ventures extended into land, cattle, agricultural products, and a variety of other endeavors. Now he was criticizing himself for not thinking big enough.

Unusual?

Not at all. That is a common characteristic of those people who burst from the multitude and demonstrate a dimension of life unthinkable to most others.

Ben Feldman will be remembered as a legend in the insurance business, an industry in which only about 5 percent of the agents exceed annual sales of $1 million. Ben Feldman sold more than eighty times that amount in one year. His lifetime sales exceeded $1 billion.

"What is the difference between you and the agents selling a million dollars in one year?" I once asked him. "Are you eighty times better than they are?"

"Not at all," he replied. "The average person just doesn't think big enough."

His advice to others reflects that. Speaking before thousands, this superstar from East Liverpool, Ohio, was known for statements like these:

"Don't be afraid to dream big dreams."

"Let go of lower things and reach for higher."

Controlling the Mind

These people whose thinking is bigger than others have unlocked a mental capacity to go beyond the doubts and limitations of the ordinary mind. For example, one warm August evening a wiry 107-pound man from India named Ramananda sat on the floor of an auditorium at the University of Minnesota. Dr. O. P. Tiwari of Chicago was describing him. "Don't forget he's sixty-eight. He's a medical miracle. He's done five thousand push-ups nonstop."

A chain with links of half-inch-thick steel was brought out. "Come and try to pull it apart," Tiwari said to the audience. Ten people, five on each end, had no effect on it. "It's been tested by metallurgists," advised Tiwari.

Then the six-foot chain was wrapped around Ramananda's waist, strung between his bent legs, and connected to a metal bar under his feet. "You will now see what can happen if the mind is under control," Dr. Tiwari announced.

The spindly little man, sitting on the floor, braced himself against the bar under his feet. His body tensed, then his legs plunged forward. The chain broke in the middle of a link!

Impossible? Of course it would be for the vast majority of people. Not because of chains around their bodies, but because of the chains around their minds. Their doubts, skepticism, and fears form the links that bind their thoughts.

Or, as Ben Feldman would say, "The average person just doesn't think big enough."

The term *big thinking* has been bandied about in business and sales circles for years. A lot of people using the words never lay out the specifics. Unless those thoughts are backed by some kind of demonstrated skill or resourcefulness, they are little more than smoke in the wind, fluff, and can lead to heartache and futility.

Notice that both Feldman and Simplot did not comprehend the consequence of big thinking until each had tucked away a fairly enviable portion of success. Perhaps that is a characteristic of valid big thinking. For it to have purpose and vigor it must become reality by *doing* after the picture is formed in the mind.

To convert big thoughts to building blocks of the future, start with one success. It need not be large or impressive. Just one little ordinary, everyday success will do. Then make sure that the next one is a wee bit larger than the last.

Now you're ready to apply big thinking that will take you somewhere secure and satisfying. Rock-solid, motivating big thinking is piling up enough victories in your life to make you aware that you have the ability to accomplish more in the days ahead.

Each one of those accomplishments will prepare you for the next, and they will expand in size and importance according to your own growth and desire.

Like others who have gathered a fair number of the prizes of life, you will probably look back someday and say, "I didn't think big enough." But for now, don't let that muddle your objectives. Just go out today and do a little bit better than yesterday.

The Birth of Big Thinking

If big thinking could find an origin, it would probably be with the birth of Orison Swett Marden in 1850. Orphaned at seven, he learned to get ahead by reading a book titled *Self-Help.*

By the time he had worked his way through Boston University and Harvard, he had fostered a catering business and saved nearly $20,000. With this he acquired an old tourist hotel near Newport, Rhode Island.

At that time, Newport was the playground of the rich, each one trying to outdo the other's mansion. Marden became convinced that the celebrated and wealthy got there by a method rather than luck or genius. So he interviewed Carnegie, Edison, Rockefeller, and others who had achieved fame.

There was a style of thinking, he found, that had led the great ones to success. He applied those principles to his own life. His perseverance, self-discipline, singleness of purpose, and positive thinking led to his ownership of five hotels.

More important to him, however, was sharing his discoveries through a manuscript he wrote, *Pushing to the Front.* A severe test of his tenacity occurred on a night in 1892. One of his hotels, Marden's Midway Hotel, in Kearney, Nebraska, burned to the ground. With it went the manuscript of his book.

The great depression of that time had just started rolling; it swept away the rest of his hotel holdings. Undaunted, he rented a scanty room over a stable, lived on $1.50 a week, and rewrote his book.

By the time he finished, business conditions had sunk to the doldrums. No publisher would risk printing the book.

Finally, in 1894, some friends rallied about the unquenchable will of Marden and got his book published. It was an instant success and went on to 250 printings, was translated into many foreign languages, and became known the world over as a handbook for success.

Marden wrote forty more books in his lifetime. Each carried much the same theme: you can if you think you can. His philosophy was more than positive thinking. The size, intensity, depth of conviction, and focus of thinking were emphasized.

He defined, in a way, what is bandied about in a rather

loose fashion today as big thinking. Think big to win, to stand out from the crowd, to do big things.

Money Is Not the Difference

What is big thinking? How do you become a big thinker? Of one thing you can be certain: you must depart from the obsession with material possessions. Become more concerned with your standards of thinking than your standard of living.

Henry Ford, whose thinking was of considerable consequence, said, "If money is your only hope for independence, you will never have it."

John D. Rockefeller, Sr., giant innovator of financial concepts, declared: "One who starts out with the idea of getting rich won't succeed; you must have a larger ambition."

A study of eighty-five millionaires in the 1970s revealed that not one had aspired to gaining wealth. All were motivated by dreams beyond personal gain.

The very nature of the quest for money dwarfs the larger potentials of thought. Concentration is centered on scarcity, loss, and security. Worry is expended on whether or not one is getting enough of what one perceives as being limited.

In a biography of the notable big thinker Albert Einstein, *An Intimate Study of a Great Man*, was written: "While Albert Einstein is encased in a human body, and it is true that he eats and drinks and laughs and talks just as a human, he thinks in terms of the universe. And because he does this the man and his thought are a closed preserve to a matter world."

Big thinking is rising above the trivia of the material world. It is knowing that what is held in the mind is largely illusions that narrow the possibilities of the human spirit. We must set these illusions aside to think of the nobler purposes of life.

Big thinkers do not necessarily follow the paths of others. They go, instead, where there is no path and leave a trail!

Your life is simply an extension of your thinking. The dimensions of your life are in direct proportion to the dimensions of your thinking.

That's why it's good advice to think big.

Thinking big means filling your mind with as much hope, as many dreams, the richest expectations, and the most positive thoughts possible and then holding them there hour after hour, day after day, month after month, and year after year.

Successful people are big thinkers. They have been able to construct such priceless qualities of thinking as these:

1. *Big thinkers think big about people.*
Big thinkers relate to the positive, rather than negative, characteristics of others. They have faith in humanity. They hold the conviction that people have the power to rise above their failures. They see the strength, the good, the talent, the worth, the noble qualities of each person whose life they touch.

2. *Big thinkers look past today.*
All big thinkers have a big dream or a lofty goal. This carries them through the day-to-day discouragement, problems, and struggles of the little tasks.

They have the big vision to keep them going.

The big thinker stays alive and enthusiastic each day through the vision of an accomplished dream. The big thinker can see that the small chore is the seed of a realized dream.

A journey of ten thousand miles starts with one step.

Each oak tree began as an acorn. And so Firestone started over his kitchen stove. Henry Ford began in his garage. And the Mayo Clinic took roots in a country doctor's office.

The big thinkers realize that doing a little each day to build their careers represents taking the stepping-stones to the fulfillment of the big dream. They persist and endure, sustained by the promise that tomorrow offers.

3. *Big thinkers are motivated by success.*
Big thinkers are affected more by their successes than by their failures.

The inspiration from the sale overwhelms the discouragement from the turndowns; the enthusiasm of the successful is more contagious than the discouragement of the person who gives up.

So the big thinkers live, breathe, think, and act only success.

4. *Big thinkers see opportunity all around them.*
A number of years ago Dr. Russell Conwell gave a lecture entitled "Acres of Diamonds," so inspiring he was asked to give it more than five thousand times. He described a Persian farmer who dreamed of owning a diamond mine. He sold his farm and wandered through the East, into Europe, and ended up, wretched and poor, drowning himself on a seashore in Spain.

Ironically, the man who bought the farm was watering his camel one day and noticed a shimmering object in the stream. It turned out to be a diamond. Further search produced virtually "acres of diamonds."

The point was that there are "acres of diamonds" right where you are. You have the opportunity to become successful right where you are with your own skill, energy, and natural ability.

Big thinkers see this.

5. *Big thinkers have big values.*
Big thinkers have established specific concrete values by which they can make decisions and guide their lives. A person with no values is like a ship with no course.

Values such as integrity, respect for others, personal

standards of conduct, and contributions to society are examples of the beacons that have guided the progress of
humanity for ages.

With them lives have meaning. Without them life is
merely an existence.

Big thinkers know this.

"Think big" is good advice for most anyone, isn't it?

5

The World Needs Your Dreams

There was a woman, who, during World War II, went to live with her husband in camp on the Mojave Desert in New Mexico. She soon grew to hate the place. The 125-degree weather was unbearable. There was nothing in sight but monotonous sand and scrubby vegetation.

In desperation, she wrote to her parents in Ohio that she was coming home. Her father was quick to respond by airmail with only two short lines:

"Two men looked out from prison bars. One saw mud; the other saw stars."

The words caused her to think and to change her attitude! She looked at the desert and saw quaint, fragile flowers struggling to survive. She climbed over her own despair and looked into the hearts of those about her and found friendship and love. Her vision began to match the vastness and magnificence of her surroundings.

She eventually wrote a book about the country and her deep appreciation for it. Her world had not changed. But her attitude toward it had.

She learned to see the stars!

People who look beyond the muck and mire of their existence, who fasten their eyes on the stars, and then rise each morning to the level of their vision, inspire and enthuse others.

There are those who endure the torments and agonies of the day-to-day pursuit of excellence, spending grueling hours striving incessantly for the stars they have fixed in their mind's eye every waking moment.

Then, when they achieve their dreams, the world comes alive with the exhilaration of the moment.

If you look to the stars, pick one out, hitch a dream to it, nurture it, and hold it close to your heart, you will find yourself oblivious to the swamps of failure and despair that seem to surround so many lives.

What do you see through the windows of your senses, stars or mud?

For what you see you will most certainly experience!

Get a Dream

People, in a way, are like the cryptobiotic tardigrade, one of the weirdest creatures known. It can exist for more than a hundred years in a state that, by most definitions, would be called death, withdrawn in its spiny shell without water, oxygen, or heat. Yet, when it is moistened, it immediately springs back to life, the legs and head poking out from its coffinlike bony crust.

People's lives can flatten out, seem routine and dull. Like the tardigrade, they go into their shells and become shielded from the adventure of life. For them the moisture that brings back life is an untried dream, a fresh goal. Their perspectives need laundering with renewed vision.

Dream Something New

There's hope, promise, exhilaration with that thought. Off with the old, on with the new!

That focuses on an invigorating quality of the human being. There seems to be, prancing within the heart of every person, a glittering desire for the new.

Think, for a moment, of the highs of your life. Don't they have something to do with a new experience, an adventure, a new face at the door, a fresh pathway to be tried?

The first day on the job. An untried recipe. Poking around in the woods. Building a budding friendship. Traveling to strange places. An unwrapped gift waiting to be opened. The honeymoon. Moving to another home. A recent acquaintance who sparks your emotions. The first week of school. Adventure. Exploration. Growth. Change. That's what lights up your life!

The Risk of Trying

Why isn't every day like that? There are many reasons. First, there is a risk in seeking the new. It's like seating people on hard stools around the wall of a dark room for a few hours. Tell them there is a more comfortable chair somewhere in the room. Only the most adventuresome will stir, for it means groping in the blackness, stumbling, falling, crawling to find something that will make the next hours more enjoyable. Worse than the physical frustration, however, would be the laughter, jeers, and criticism of those who remain on the stools. They would rather endure the barren, uncomfortable existence that they know, chiding the one who leaves them, than venture into the unknown.

That's life. Many are sitting in boredom or despair, suppressing the quest for newness, denouncing, ridiculing, and criticizing those few who choose to break out of the routine.

Does this mean that you have to split with your mate, keep changing jobs, and switch cars and homes every year to satisfy the urge for the new? Not at all. That's just immaturity. To experience the spirited fulfillment of exploring the new, start with yourself.

A new skill! A new feeling! A new insight! A new way of looking at the world! That's the joy of newness! It's something you grow into rather than something you hope will happen to you. It starts with gazing in rather than out!

From there it can go to your relationships. Look beyond yesterday and accept the change that is always occurring as something new and exciting. It is a human paradox that you seldom love anything without seeking to alter it and, having done that, find that it is no longer what you started out loving.

But that can be marvelously stimulating. For you don't have to search out new objects for your love. Simply explore the dimensions of the loves you already have.

Dreams Bring Hope

If you aren't getting as big a jolt as you'd like from life, get yourself a dream. You are the only expression of life that has that ability. It is, in fact, your ultimate obligation.

Where there is no hope, no higher direction or noble purpose toward which a life is growing, life's current is, for all meaningful purposes, not flowing.

Other forms of life have the dreams built in. An acorn will someday become an oak tree, the wheat seed will flourish into golden grain, the lion cub will undeniably grow to be king of the jungle. How about you? What will be your destiny? It will be a realization of your dreams.

Be brave with your dreams! Don't wait for someone else to do it before you dream it!

Robert Peary aspired to be the first to set foot on the North Pole. Scottish explorer Alexander Mackenzie wanted to do what no American had done—cross the continent on foot. Nellie Bly dreamed of being the first woman to go around the world alone. The world needs dreamers like that. Organizations need them.

People who look beyond the limitations of their lives, fasten their thoughts on their dreams, and then rise each morning to the levels of their visions make miracles happen.

Your dreams are the wings of your thoughts; they lift

your thinking out of the commonplace and ordinary. Belief and dedication motivate, but dreams inspire!

Your dreams of tomorrow will make today's problems seem unimportant. The crumbs on the floor, the worn-out tire, the corn on the toe, the complaints of the customer, and the dreary turndowns will fall from your thoughts like dried leaves from a tree if you have a big dream.

Dreams take the dullness out of work, the aggravation from problems, and the hopelessness from lack.

So hold fast to your dreams! They are the harps of the heart that add music to your everyday existence!

The World Needs You

Don't give up on your dreams. The world needs them.

In the 1800s, James Allen, from his cottage on the English coast, wrote:

> The dreamers are the saviors of the world.
>
> Humanity cannot forget its dreamers; it cannot let their trials fade and die; it lives in them; it knows them as the realities which it shall one day see and know.
>
> Cherish your visions; cherish your ideals; cherish the music that stirs in your heart, the beauty that forms in your mind, the loveliness that drapes your purest thoughts. Out of them will grow all delightful conditions, all heavenly environment. Of them, if you but remain to them, your world will at last be built.
>
> Dream lofty dreams, and as you dream, so shall you become.

Modern psychologists have done little but reaffirm Allen's intuitive philosophies. James Garfield, president of Performance Sciences Institute, spent two decades studying the characteristics of fifteen hundred superachievers.

Peak performance, he found, begins with a mission. Without a dream, a compelling inner urge, life becomes a workaday routine. And that is acceptable for many, but not the dreamers.

Having a dream and then having the tenacity to stick to it longer than anyone else are more important to success than innate ability or raw talent, Garfield reports.

Dreamers Don't Give Up

What he doesn't mention is that the dreamers have little choice except to abide with their visions. For the dreamers do not know how to give up. That's right. They literally do not know how to give up. They know how to plod, grub, sacrifice, grind, and strive, but they do not know how to give up.

That quality is not easily understood by others, whose lives are spiced with a variety of interests, jobs, or pursuits. They may look at the dreamers as a stubborn lot who refuse to, don't want to, or are too naive to give up. Perhaps, to some extent, that is true. But of greater influence is that to dreamers giving up is like flying to the moon or juggling a dozen oranges; they simply do not know how to do it.

Failure does not occur to the visionary. The efforts, trials, and methods might fail, but not the dreams. In fact, failure endows the dreamer with a sense of exhilaration, as if it were a stepping-stone toward the realization of the goal.

Thomas Edison expressed this once when asked, "Mr. Edison, you have failed over a thousand times in your attempt to develop a filament for the light bulb. When are you going to give up or stop trying?"

"I haven't failed a thousand times," the inventor replied. "I've only discovered a thousand ways it can't be done."

That is somewhat like the small boy playing sandlot baseball.

His father came by and called out, "How are you doing, Tommy? What's the score?"

"Nineteen to nothing," the boy replied.

"Whose favor?" asked Dad.

"Theirs!" was the response.

"You're really being clobbered, aren't you, Tommy?" cried the father.

"Shucks no, Dad. We ain't even been to bat yet!" answered Tommy.

The Power of Dreams

So, a dream reduces the day's obstacles and setbacks to insignificance. When many are driven to sleepless nights and knotted stomachs by reverses and hardships, the dreamer is at peace. The rainbows and mountaintops rest within the soul of the dreamer. The crevices and boulders are only adornments along the way to the vision.

A dreamer is little concerned with details or methods. Let others become ensnared in those. A dreamer knows there are many pathways to a destination. If one leads to a dead end, then another will be found.

To the person who aspires to a vision, each day is more elevated than the one before. It is this knowledge in the heart of the dreamer that makes life a constant ascent toward the stars.

Dreams are like those stars. They will never be touched, but they become guides in darkness. Following them will ensure that your destiny will be reached.

So find a dream. Keep it, nurture it, hold it close to your heart. To let it go is to die; your spirit shrivels.

Dreams enthuse; they erase dullness from your life. Verily they become life itself.

Your life will be measured by the size of your dreams!

6

The Life-Changing Power of Goals

The beginning of a new year is the time when people look forward, with hope, expectancy, and wonder, to the future events of their lives. Some will plan. Some will make New Year's resolutions.

In spite of these good intentions, however, life will tick on pretty much the same way for the vast majority. Because most people are just about where they really want to be. They have spent their lives in trial and error, seeking comfortable situations, avoiding unpleasant conditions, until they have established a routine and a position for themselves that they can tolerate. They often wish or daydream that life would be more adventurous and exciting. However, in spite of these thoughts, life never seems to change much.

There is a reason why life is like this, why life extends itself into the future the same way it has been in the past. (Thoreau said, "The mass of men lead lives of quiet desperation.") There is also a reason why, for a very few people, life will be dramatically different in the future.

The reason is the same for all. It is simple. It can be stated in just one word. Goals!

Everyone Has Goals

Goals shape people's lives. Sometimes they appear first as
dreams or visions. But regardless of the name you put on
them, they add up to the same influence. They determine
the courses of people's destinies, molding circumstances
and eventually the inner characteristics of attitude, thought,
and feeling.

You hear a good deal about goals. The amount of
advice you receive about the wisdom of setting goals is
unlimited. Occasionally you notice an individual of unusual achievement whose success is attributed to setting
goals. That, of course, is true. But not unusual.

For all people set goals. Their everyday existence is
regulated by their goals. People start living by goals very
early in life. Usually their parents started setting their goals
for them: Go to school. Work hard. Be good. Get a job.
Raise children. Once implanted, such fundamentals have
never changed.

Along the way, however, most pick up many other
goals: Impress others. Watch TV. Socialize. Take things
easy. Avoid failure. Don't get involved with too many
things. Look around for ways to make more money. Change
jobs. Spend time with family or friends. Get a hobby.

The list is endless. In fact it is so long that goals
become the primary source of conflict and frustration in
people's lives. If you are one of the rare few who want to
make an effort to remove this anxiety from your life, use
the talents and abilities you have to your advantage to make
goals work for you instead of against you.

Lives Are Like Ships

A ship without a pilot or course would drift aimlessly about
the sea, being driven by the waves and wind, eventually
ending up a wreck on some barren shore.

A human life is not much different. Without direction

and purpose and a mind firmly in control, fate and circumstances alone will determine one's destiny.

No individual need sacrifice his or her life to such
chance and happenstance, however. For the human being,
apart from all other forms of life, is given the power to
choose the paths of existence.

Journeys through life can be charted, planned, and
experienced by the intellect and will of the individual. The
process begins with setting destinations or goals. That is
apparently life's ultimate purpose.

For the human being is a goal-seeking mechanism.
Life's greatest meaning is achieved when one is reaching
out and striving for a goal. If days are filled with emptiness
and despair, it is because there are no inspiring goals. Yes,
goals must be inspiring, filling the heart with hope and
excitement.

How Your Future Is Created

Everyone has goals. People know exactly where they
choose to be because of their goals. A vagrant wanders
about the street, penniless, seeking only food and a place
to sleep. Those have become the only daily goals. Not lofty
goals, of course, but goals nonetheless.

You know people who are chasing from morning 'til
night, busy as kittens in a yarn basket and not accomplish-
ing much more. Each task, each errand started as a deliberately chosen goal, eventually becoming a series of habits.
Confusion and chaos are then a way of life.

All of these lives could be lifted from mediocrity by
following the advice of Frank Lloyd Wright, the famed
American architect. He is credited with saying, "Make no
little plans, for there is no magic in them to stir people's
souls."

His plans were blueprints that started as dreams. Then
the dreams became goals. So, make no little goals, for there
is no energy in them to empower you to the larger dimen-

sions of life. Most people are letting dozens and dozens of trivial goals and habits dominate their day-to-day lives. Where they will be five and ten years from now is simply an extension of where they are today.

Goals Fuel Achievement

If you would dare break out of self-imposed boundaries, you must do it by setting goals. They can be realistic and achievable as long as they are constantly progressing. As one level is realized, another a bit higher is established.

That is the thrill and excitement of the unlimited nature of life—always reaching out and achieving a new and higher goal. That is also the only way to discover the invisible greatness within you.

Many people won't admit that exists. They see themselves as quite average and not rising much above what they are now.

Forget about what you have done or holding yourself back when setting goals.

It is always amazing to witness the transformation in people's lives when they learn how to use goals. For a goal held in the mind, nurtured, and stimulated by desire will inevitably change the person.

It is a known fact that setting goals is one of the requisites for achievement and success. Goals concentrate energy, direct effort, establish priorities, facilitate planning, and provide a means of measuring progress. But there is another dimension to goal setting that contributes to performance accomplishments that is rarely mentioned. It is an intangible characteristic that is difficult to predict but always prevails.

Once you establish a clear-cut goal and let it install itself firmly in your mind, almost automatically, and often in remote and unexplainable ways, you start attracting those things in your life that contribute to reaching your goal.

Some testify that it is the mysterious process of

thought becoming reality. Some attribute it to "luck." However, in a study once done on people who were consistently and often incredibly "lucky," it was found that they set goals and were always exposing themselves to situations that were goal-connected. On the other hand, people who were "unlucky" had no goals.

Goals for Power

New talents, unknown abilities, and fresh enthusiasm will blossom from a mind opened by the pursuit of a goal. The person will proclaim excitedly, "I have discovered I can do something I never knew I could do before."

The individual will have been awakened by a new-found power that need never be exhausted as the boundless potentials of life are explored. This process, be assured, is not fantasy or motivational vaccination. Experiences like this are well-documented events that have occurred in the lives of people like you.

It starts in the human mind with a determination to "make no little plans."

7

How to Get Where You Want to Go

In a small suburban community in the Midwest, a parade of children was marching through the main street of the town. Suddenly a car raced up from behind the parade, plowed through the children, bounded from a parked car, cut a devastating swath through onlookers, and finally wrecked itself against a lamppost. Result: two killed, several severely injured. Later it was found that the driver had suffered a heart attack and died at the wheel. The car had had no driver.

It was, of course, a tragedy. But it was a tragedy that is occurring millions of times—*Daily!* People are running their lives with no driver, no course, with some devastating results.

If people operated their automobiles the way most operate their lives, they would never get out of the driveway. Fortunately, their cars are operated with more prudence. Before they start driving, they anticipate where they want to go: they have a destination. If they don't know how to get to their destination, they consult a map.

Then they sit in the driver's seat. They fasten their seat belts. They start the motor, check the gas supply, place their hands on the steering wheel, and then guide the auto to their destination along a predetermined course at a predetermined rate of speed.

The same principles are involved in conducting your life. To get from one point to another in life, all you have to do is to operate your life as you would any other vehicle.

The formula is so amazingly simple that it is almost unbelievable that many lives are ended without ever getting out of the garage; many more people get out of the garage but end up wrecked or lost in some desolate area.

Let's reexamine the driving principles to orient them to your attitudes and life:

1. *Decide on your destination.*
How can you expect your life to have direction if you don't know where you're going? How can you accomplish something if you don't know what you want to accomplish?

Do you start out in your car without deciding where you want to go? You might say "Yes, sometimes." You can do exactly the same thing with your life if that is what you want.

You can "go for a ride." You can start out and just roll along, looking at the scenery, passing time, and then come back to the same place you started. But if this is how you choose to spend your life, don't blame people, circumstances, or "the system" for not taking you to a destination of prosperity and recognition.

On the other hand, you can go as far as you like if you set your destination, allow the time, and put your plan into operation.

But you must decide on your destination and set your goals! After you have set your goals, how much you can accomplish with your life will be incredible. For those who understand the powerful influence of goals, it is never any great surprise when phenomenal results are achieved.

Guglielmo Marconi decided at the age of twelve that he was going to be the inventor of wireless telegraphy. He established this goal in spite of the fact that famed scientists of his time had been unable to achieve it.

Jonas Salk established a goal of conquering polio. Henry Ford aimed his efforts at creating a horseless carriage. The Wright brothers set a goal of flying.

When John Goddard was fifteen years old, he made a list of all the things he wanted to do. He set down 127 goals, among them to climb Mt. Everest, explore the Nile, study primitive tribes in the Sudan, circumnavigate the globe, run a five-minute mile, dive in a submarine, read the Bible from cover to cover, play "Claire de Lune" on the piano, write a book, read the entire *Encyclopaedia Britannica.* Idle dreaming? Not to Goddard. Now tough and middle-aged, he has become one of the most famous explorers in the world. At last count, Goddard had accomplished 105 of his original 127 goals. Still to go: visit all 141 countries of the world (he's been to only 113 so far), explore the entire Yangtze River, live to see the twenty-first century (he'll be seventy-five), and visit the moon.

Goals, whether they are achieved or not, change the individual. Goals channel mental resources toward a specific objective.

Research reveals that people who set goals are happier, earn more money, and have more successful job records than those with no goals.

In one study of Yale University graduates who had been out of school for twenty years, 3 percent had taken the time to write down their goals and change them as they went along. Ten percent of the graduates knew what they wanted to do and could talk about it in broad terms. Eighty-seven percent of the graduates had never bothered to write down their goals. The result of twenty years showed that the 3 percent achieved more than the other 97 percent combined.

After you have selected your goal, transpose it into a "power picture." One of the most vivid ways to do this is to create a "Goal Book." You can use any scrapbook or notebook. In the front of your "Goal Book," write down your goal. Then find pictures that illustrate achieving your goal.

If your goal is to earn more money, find pictures of the

things you will buy with it. If your goal is to remodel your home, find pictures of the way it will look after remodeling.

The more firmly these pictures become implanted in your mind, the more powerful will be the effect on your behavior and life. But make the decision now . . . that you will bring new meaning to your life by following the plan outlined here for setting and picturing goals.

2. *Plan the route.*
American industrialist Henry Kaiser said, "Know yourself and decide what you want most out of life. Then write down your goals and a plan to reach them." Develop a plan, utilizing all of the known facilities, abilities, knowledge, and energies that you have at your command for achieving your goal.

The first thing you will discover is this: a big goal must be broken down into a number of small goals. That's the secret of harnessing the tremendous power potential that you have. Each of the small parts can then be achieved as a short-range goal.

Most people will not establish a large goal, because they wilt at the thought of the total effort involved. The National Institute of Standards and Technology tells us that a dense fog covering seven city blocks, a hundred feet deep, is composed of something less than one glass of water. The glass of water is divided into some sixty billion tiny drops. Yet those tiny drops of water can blot out practically all vision.

The same is true of you! Your effort, broken into small quantities, applied daily toward one objective, can create a huge impression. But then the activities must be mobilized, brought together, and focused.

One day an efficiency expert named Ivy Lee was discussing his services with Charles Schwab, then president of Bethlehem Steel.

Lee handed Schwab a blank sheet of paper and said, "Write down the six most important tasks you have to do tomorrow."

After Schwab had done this, Lee said, "Now number them in the order of their importance." Again, Schwab complied.

"Now," Lee explained, "put that paper in your pocket. Tomorrow, open it and start working on the most important task. Stick with it until it is completed. Then start on the second, then go on to the third, fourth, and then the fifth. Don't become concerned if you don't finish all six. You will always be working on the most important task.

"Do this every day," Lee advised. "Use it as long as you wish and then send me a check for what you think it is worth."

In a few weeks, Charles Schwab sent Ivy Lee a check for $25,000 and a letter explaining that the idea was the most valuable he had ever learned. In five years this plan helped turn Bethlehem Steel into the world's biggest independent steel producer. And it helped Schwab make $100 million!

After you have broken your master goal into small daily elements, you can apply this system to your goal progress. When you list the six most important things you have to do the next day, keep uppermost the accomplishment of your ultimate goal. That, then, becomes a daily priority.

3. *Stay on the route.*
Check your progress from time to time. Stay with your plan every day.

Many people go speeding along the highways of life in a hurry to go nowhere. They are like the fellow driving from New York to Miami who decided to take a shortcut. Hours later, his wife consulted a map.

"Herman," she said, "I'm afraid we're lost."

"So who cares?" he said as he sped along the highway. "We're making great time!"

Write down your goals and visualize them. Then prepare a plan for achieving them. Break this down into daily activities.

Select the six most important things you have to do the next day and then arrange them in the order of their importance. At the beginning of each day, start working on the most important thing.

This plan will save you from being pulled in the direction of the least important activity. You are always waylaid by grocery shopping, a few minutes for a cup of coffee, a television program, time-consuming details, or the parasites of trivia. You need a plan such as this to be constantly working on the most important segment of your goal.

The difference between you and the multimillionaire may not be brains, education, desire, or ambition—but planning.

Make sure you're developing the best possible plan to reach your destination. Ask for opinions, investigate the plans of others who have achieved goals similar to yours, and do any research necessary to help you create the best plan. After all, you would not purposely start for a destination over dirt roads and detours when a four-lane freeway was available, would you?

So, to sum up steps 2 and 3: (a) Plan your route. (b) Make sure you can reach your destination by some route. If not, revise your destination. (c) Investigate all possible routes to make sure you have the best route. Then . . .

4. *Get in the driver's seat.*
Many fail to achieve their dreams, hopes, or goals because they never get themselves or anybody else in the driver's seat. Did you ever see a car, ship, plane, or bus in motion without a driver or pilot? It just is not possible, is it? In other words, get yourself in the best possible position to achieve your goal.

Perhaps you don't know how to drive. In other words, you need someone's help to achieve your goal. In that case, get that other person in the driver's seat.

This is where many bog down. They do not want to put someone else in the driver's seat for fear that person will receive the recognition.

Charles Rumley, president of General Motors of Canada, once said, "There is almost no end to what we can accomplish if we don't care who gets the credit!"

Regardless of whether it is you or someone else, that driver's seat must be occupied by someone who knows the destination, the course, and how to operate the vehicle.

5. *Check the fuel supply.*

Find out what you need to know to achieve your goal. Do you have enough knowledge, information, skill, and ability? You would hardly start a long trip and expect to get there on an empty gas tank, would you? Neither would you expect to become the chef at a Hyatt Hotel if you knew nothing about cooking.

So check your supply of fuel to make sure you have enough to get started. Notice I said "get started"—not get to your destination.

Many never get started toward a destination because they feel they have to store up enough fuel to last them to the end of the trip.

With the availability of fueling stations in the world in the form of experts, correspondence courses, institutions, libraries, training programs, and specialized books, refueling along the way to your destination is not a problem. When the journey is long, it becomes a necessity.

Check your fuel supply to make sure you have enough to get started. Then plan on refueling regularly.

6. *Start moving.*

How many ideas, aspirations, intents, and dreams have you had that never materialized?

Know why? Very simple. You were distracted by a tempting, brutish little ghoul named "Procrastination."

Ask your friend, Noah Webster, about him. He will say, "Oh, yes. He almost kept me from finishing my dictionary. For thirty-six years I battled him, from the time I started until I finished. He encouraged me to put off my work from day to day. He comes from a large family. I know his sisters named Defer, Delay, Retard, Postpone and Prolong. He also has three little brothers named Tarry, Dawdle and Dally."

And, friend, if he gets into the front seat of that car with you, you will never get out of the driveway! You will never get in motion with Procrastination along! Why not rid yourself of him?

Get the vehicle moving to get to your destination. The idea is expressed in this Chinese proverb: "A journey of a thousand miles must begin with a single step."

7. *Follow the route.*
Now work your plan—day after day. Stay on the route you've established.

Calvin Coolidge said this: "Nothing in the world can take the place of persistence. Talent will not; nothing is more common than unsuccessful people with talent. Genius will not; unrewarded genius is almost a proverb. Education will not; the world is full of educated derelicts. Persistence and determination alone are omnipotent!"

You cannot abandon your vehicle and get to your destination. Neither can you change courses, going in the opposite direction, and expect to reach your destination.

If the vehicle breaks down, you have to repair it and then get going again. If a bridge is washed out, take a detour. But then get back on the route! Be determined to follow the route, day after day, to arrive at your destination.

This is your action program to apply all that you have learned about goal setting. Before leaving our analogy of life and a journey, let's briefly observe some of the safety rules:

8. *Drive safely.*
   • Drive slowly. Speed is unimportant. Just keep moving. Driving at a reckless speed can put you in a ditch and can even mean a loss of life.
   • Shortcuts can be costly. After selecting the route you're convinced is the shortest and most practical, stick to it. If you start out over plowed fields

or rocky hills to save a few miles, you're going to end up walking or giving up the trip. Quick money and easy rewards are usually just tempting shortcuts that will delay your journey.

• Respect other drivers. You will acquire the respect and friendship of others, as well as personal satisfaction, by respecting the rights and feelings of others while driving to your destination. You do not reach worthwhile goals in spite of other people; you reach them because of other people.

• Allow plenty of time. Give yourself ample time to reach your destination. Realize that you are only a human being and you need rest, relaxation, and enjoyment along the way. Give yourself plenty of time to take breaks, enjoy the company of others, eliminate fatigue, and obtain pleasure from your journey.

• Observe the laws and signs. There are two ways to drive—the right way and the wrong way. You can observe the signs, follow the rules, and achieve your destination within the structure of the laws, either written or unwritten. The laws were not conceived to restrict you but to help you. Respect the signs and the rules. If you do, you will not be delayed by arrests and accidents; you will be assured of reaching your destination.

8

Stay Focused

In a few blunt paragraphs the morning paper announced the bankruptcy of a previously successful local entrepreneur. The article was a bleary epitaph to a once-brilliant career crushed by a senseless ego.

The individual was, at heart, a grocery man. From a small start, he assembled an impressive chain of stores. But then he became involved with a variety of enterprises quite different from the neighborhood convenience stores he had fashioned so expertly.

He lost his focus, and in doing so he lost all that he had gained.

It is a tragically familiar story that occurs constantly. Years ago I helped a fellow get into real estate. His had been a nomadic existence of wandering from one thing to another, always hoping to strike it rich.

"This is it," he told me. "I've been jumping around enough. I'm going to stick to real estate no matter what happens." In a short time he was reasonably successful. But that lasted only a few months. He quit, apologetically explaining he had been offered a distributorship for a new-fangled product for babies.

I heard from him occasionally over the following

years. Each time he was in a hot new deal that supposedly would be better than owning a gold mine. It never happened. He finally died quite suddenly, frustrated, confused, and burdened by debt. He was never able to bring his talents, abilities, and ambitions into focus.

A more recent case was a friend who helped build an organization that provided him with exceptional earnings. But then he fell into a fault-finding mood and began wandering from one endeavor to another, assuming that success would follow him.

Unable to bring his activities into focus, he ended up in the oblivion of bankruptcy. The simple process of bankruptcy is always the finale to a sad story of trauma and frustration as a life sinks into despair. The cause, in most instances, is the same—lack of focus.

Many careers are woefully limited because they do not remain focused. Examine the lives of those who have lifted themselves from a bare-bones existence to wealth or fame, and you will find they got there by staying focused. They picked out a goal, a purpose, an endeavor, and then stuck to it doggedly. They learned how to be effective and then concentrated their efforts, thoughts, and talents on the product or service that was their focus.

Resist Distractions

Your dedication is always challenged after you achieve a certain level of success. When the world discovers that you're moderately successful, you're approached by all sorts of dealers in fairy dust, ticky-tacky opportunities, and overnight wealth. There are those with their little satchels of the latest, hottest deals who would lure you into helping them make money by your efforts.

Internally that tiny squeaky voice is chiding you: "Maybe there is an easier way to make money. This could be a big opportunity. Why not try it? You can always continue what you're doing."

No, you can't. You lose your focus, energy, loyalty,

drive, and commitment. You lose all that has brought you success. From there it's an erosive process of finding fault and condemning what you've been doing.

It is wise to remind ourselves that it is not the product or service, the compensation plan, the company, or any other outside characteristic that makes us successful. Success is not an external force; it is internal. It is that quality of bringing our talents, energy, and dedication into focus and keeping them there.

Those who have that ability are never casting about for elusive opportunity. They have found it within themselves. They realize that there will be ultimate financial security in whatever they choose to do, whether it's a trade, a skill, or a profession, whether it's selling pencils or skyscrapers.

The lesson is clear. Avoid the demons of distraction. Stay focused!

When Focus Is Lost

Companies stop expanding.

Marriages stop being fun and exciting.

People stop growing.

Salespeople stop increasing their sales.

Even the ambitious and hopeful stop getting ahead in their careers.

There's one reason, more overwhelming than any other, that retards this forward momentum of individuals and organizations.

It's this. People get so busy with the results of success that they stop doing the things that made them successful.

They lose their focus.

New Ventures Have Focus

The venturesome get together with an idea, a dream, a stake of seed money, and boundless energy to start a business. The days are not long enough to contain their vigor. They'll stand on their head for hours to see a prospect and do somersaults back to the office to fill the order correctly. No problem is too burdensome or savings too small to evade the dedicated attention of the aspiring entrepreneurs.

After long, long hours of clutching, sacrificing, being bruised and battered, the glorious day comes when the red ink becomes black! A clientele is established. Business begins flowing smoothly.

But then thought and effort are gradually diverted toward moving desks, decorating the waiting room, lining up items to talk about at the next meeting, and coordinating luncheon schedules. The priorities that once emerged from being lean and hungry receive only casual regard.

Twenty years later, if good fortune and survival principles are not entirely lacking, the owners find themselves with a nice little business thumping along at a fraction of its potential. Like being on a merry-go-round, the big dreamers of years ago find themselves seated in comfortable saddles going up and down and around and around, but always ending up in the same place. Of course. They're doing nothing that would substantially change the position of their company. That process stopped shortly after their beginning.

The Same Is True of Marriages

Let's look at marriages. Boy meets girl. The chemistry is right. Emotions tingle! Every moment is special, heart-filled with poetry, music, movies, picnics, dancing, fun, and laughter. So, with the organ playing "We've Only Just Begun," they both say, "I do."

Their eyes and good intentions say it will never change.

But it does. In a hurry. The long talks in the moonlight are replaced by TV. The filet mignon with candlelight is transformed into spaghetti and leftover casseroles. Bills must be paid, little noses wiped, grass cut, bathrooms cleaned . . . and when did all that love and affection get dumped into the garbage disposal?

Spouses go along in a dull silence, wondering to themselves why the other one doesn't do something to add a little jingle to the music of the marriage.

Assuming the odds stay on the together side, they're cutting the anniversary cake twenty-five years later with the comment "It hasn't always been easy. There have been some tough times, but we made it."

Not always easy? Tough times? Does it have to be that way? What if they had held on to all the adventuresome events and niceties that made the relationship romantic and thrilling when they first got together?

How are your relationships? Have you stopped doing the things that made them rich, meaningful, successful at the beginning?

Stay focused on the characteristics that make a marriage successful.

So, how is your life? Have you been swept along with all the trivia that a little success produces? Have you stopped doing the things that brought you just a few of the goodies? Have you lost your focus?

Focus Your Subconscious Mind

Decide what you want from life. That's the most important step in living a full, rich life.

You have within you the most magnificent mechanism in the universe—your mind. It has two parts—the conscious and the subconscious. The miraculous powers of the subconscious have never been fully realized by humanity. It is the guiding force that determines your destiny; it will attract and support whatever you want.

The subconscious mind takes its direction from the conscious mind. Identify what you want, and your subconscious mind will help you get it. A lot of people never do that. They feed conflicting directions to the subconscious. They lack focus.

They say they want success. Then they also think about going out for dinner, spending a weekend at the

lake, finding out what's on TV that evening. Doubt, criticism, and complaints filter through the mind. Remember
that the subconscious always supports the conscious. If
weeding the petunia bed is uppermost in your thoughts,
the subconscious will block out everything else and guide
you to your petunia bed. But that's not where you will find
success, is it?

Decide what you want from life. That becomes your
vision. Imagine that you are already there. Clear your mind
of all the garbage and junk that's holding you back. Clarify
your vision. Then focus on it.

Don't worry about how you will achieve your vision.
Your subconscious will guide you. The process will evolve.

The moment you decide what you want, the vision, the
dream, will follow. Hold your vision in focus and your
inner energies will become mobilized to fulfill your desire.

It is an adventuresome, exciting future that far exceeds
sitting, waiting, without a specific focus.

9

Believe and Succeed!

What makes the difference between success and failure? Why do some people have energy and drive while others are listless and drifting? Why do some people lead lives of satisfaction and accomplishment while others continually face futility and despair?

The answer lies in one magic, mysterious quality—*motivation.* Motivation is the ingredient that propels us to action. Motivation is the elusive fuel that incites us to accomplish what the mind proposes. Motivated people have drive, direction, and purpose.

Your mind can conceive success. You know how to be more successful, don't you? You can easily think of a dozen ideas that would make your life more abundant. Why aren't they put into action? Lack of motivation! Motivation is the difference—motivation sufficient to overcome fear of failure, laziness, lack of confidence, and complacency.

Your ability to make yourself move is the difference. An ancient Arabian proverb declares: "All mankind is divided into three classes: those that are immovable, those that are movable, and those that move." Honestly, now, into which class would you place yourself? This is the number-one problem of people today: making themselves move.

If you're motivated, you can achieve anything that your mind conceives. All things are possible to you! Familiar words? Delve into their meaning and the key to motivation is revealed. Ponder this for a moment: all things are possible to you if you have the ability to believe. Motivation is not wanting; it is believing.

The Key to Motivation

The ability to believe is the foundation for motivation! This is the blazing talent of all famous and successful people. History has remembered only those people who have developed the ability to believe! Belief, not reward, is the fuel that incites us to accomplish what the mind conceives.

Did Columbus face famine, disaster, and sea monsters with a gang of cutthroats because he thought it was a good deal? Did the Pilgrims face annihilation, hardship, and starvation for a pension plan? Did half-blind Johannes Kepler work a lifetime by the light of a greasy candle to chart the heavens for a shorter workweek? Did Clara Barton reach out for the problems of humanity and finally build the Red Cross for fringe benefits? Of course not!

These great, great people are examples of those powered by an ability to believe intensely, emotionally, overwhelmingly, in a spirit, a cause, a purpose, or a person. It was this ability to believe that motivated them to their great achievements.

But you too have this gift! You have the latent, smoldering spark of belief embedded within you, a spark that is waiting to be fanned into a fire of purpose, of accomplishment, of a life of abundant success!

The ability to believe is the secret of motivation. Believing is the root and fiber of enthusiasm. It is the master weaver of accomplishment, the foundation of purpose for your life.

Believing can convert your life from a drab day-to-day existence into an exciting adventure of achievement.

You Have the Power

Your ability to believe begins with a belief in yourself and the human spirit. You, as most individuals, are victimized and tormented by your weaknesses and illusions of life. But above this marsh is firm ground. There is the sacred precinct of your strength, the eternity of life, the dignity of your personality, and the heritage of your moral stature.

These are the true temples of your existence. Just as you fall, you surely shall rise. Believe that ultimately you will triumph over all that would hold you from your rewards. This must be one of the nobler purposes of your existence.

Your belief in yourself, your efforts, your future, and your God will provide the warp and woof of your life. With these threads you can weave experiences of beauty and meaning; without them you will have the snarls and knots of a patternless existence.

Know that all you see of the human scene—the hideous, the violent, the savage—is but illusion. It will pass. The magnificence of the human spirit will remain. Do not let the thorns of life deflate your belief in loving others.

Believe in nothing and you will be nothing. You will perceive others as you perceive yourself. If you do not believe in your own greatness and unlimited spirit, how can you possibly create a faith, a confidence, a trust in another?

Life is not experiencing what is left over from your pain, anger, or setbacks. Life is going ahead facing all of those conditions and feeling a deep satisfaction that you have lived beyond them. You have experienced courage and gone through whatever you had to so as to fulfill your belief in life.

Believe and Learn

While in New York once, I met a young man from Argentina who was working in the hotel where I was staying. Although he had been in this country for only two weeks, he could speak English well enough so we could communicate. He had completed a law course at the University of Buenos Aires and had started his law career in Argentina. He soon realized what a valuable asset it would be to be able to speak English fluently.

"I know there is no way to do this but to come to America and live with its people. So here I am. In Argentina I am a lawyer. Here I scrape food off dishes in the kitchen," he laughingly told me.

"But no matter," he added. "I am getting to know the people and the language. That is what I am here for."

Here was a young man who was devoting a portion of his life to traveling thousands of miles, living in a strange country with strange people, just to develop a skill that would be useful to him in his business.

"Why didn't you take English language courses at the university?" I asked.

"I did do that," he replied. "But you no really learn to speak a language without living with the people."

You don't really learn to do something with poise, confidence, and sincerity unless you get involved, do it, and believe in it. Then live it! So there you have it. That's life, squeezed down to one small incident. Have faith and belief. Remove all negative thoughts.

A Common Trait of Great People

Examine the lives of all great people in history.

They believed in themselves and in a cause or purpose. And they had faith. They had faith in people, in life, in their goals and their daily activity. If you are going to succeed in a career, you must have a certain amount of belief and faith. In fact your degree of success might very well be measured by your degree of belief and faith.

When you analyze those qualities of belief and faith, you realize why they provide the personal power to be a stand-out achiever.

To achieve you must be physically endowed with energy and drive. You must have willpower, personal motivation, confidence, enthusiasm, conviction, hope, and vision. You must be willing to face failure, rejection, and problems with no effect on your position or direction.

The lives of successful people have demonstrated that sort of perseverance.

Frank Woolworth worked hard to save his first $50 and then saw three of his first five chain stores fail. Cyrus H. K. Curtis lost more than $800,000 on the *Saturday Evening Post* before it paid a dollar of profit. Du Pont worked for eleven years and spent $27 million before the first pound of nylon was sold. Abraham Lincoln was badly defeated in five different elections and suffered one failure after another before becoming president. Bob Richards spent more than ten thousand hours practicing pole-vaulting to win a gold medal at the Olympics. There was never a bar of music that Beethoven did not rewrite a dozen times. William Cullen Bryant rewrote "Thanatopsis" a hundred times.

How do you achieve the belief that leads to such perseverance? It begins with discipline.

Transform Dreams to Belief

The human mind is a tricky mechanism that wishes, dreams, hopes, envisions, and longs for a multitude of things that will seldom be attained. From well-intentioned New Year's resolutions to the stern-jawed goal-setting process, thoughts are cast out helter-skelter to capture the hungers of the heart.

But there comes a time, whether by dismay or futility, when one must struggle with the realization that the idle wish or dogged resolution is falling woefully short of actualization.

The desire to be rich is so popular it is held almost to be evil.

For every person who achieves a goal there are a thousand who come up dismally empty-handed.

Wishes are merely threads from which frustration is woven.

All of these longings, hopes, and ambitions, for most, turn out to be fluff—wispy moods that, at best, only brighten corners of the mind.

Visions, wishes, goals, hopes—all must be wrought into sterner stuff for them to have an impact on a life.

Examine the lives of all the famous and accomplished and you will find only one shared characteristic. There are tall ones, short ones, old and young, men and women, learned and unlearned, with just one common denominator. They possess belief. They believe in themselves and what they are doing. That one quality sets them apart from the wishers and momentarily inspired goal setters.

The Results of Belief

The effect of belief is beyond the grasp of logic. I knew a man who believed he was ill. He went from doctor to doctor, none of whom could find anything wrong. My friend became less and less active, at last convinced that walking even a short block was too great an exertion.

It took him five years to do it, but he finally succumbed completely to his belief, dropping dead while being admitted to a hospital.

For every instance like that there are multitudes who are rising from sickness or setback to the higher planes of productive life powered by a positive belief.

A belief held tenaciously in the mind for a period of time will absolutely and undeniably be fulfilled in your life.

Examine your beliefs and you will forecast your destiny, for, once acquired, they will dominate your existence. Captured by a belief, you become a servant to its fulfillment.

Act Out Belief

To be consumed by the raptures of a belief is to experience life's richest joys and satisfactions. To believe in a career, purpose, person, or spiritual direction and spend day after day acting out that conviction is the ultimate realization of your potential.

Acting out, demonstrating a belief, is the prime virtue of this sort of mental dedication. It must be done if you truly believe.

The fable is told about the famed Zumbrati, who walked a tightrope across Niagara Falls. Conditions were less than ideal. It was a windy day. The performer was thankful to have made it across.

One of those waiting to congratulate him was a man with a wheelbarrow.

"I believe you could walk across pushing this wheelbarrow," the man told him.

Zumbrati shook his head and said he felt fortunate to have accomplished the feat without a wheelbarrow.

The man urged him to try. "I believe that you can do it," he said.

The aerialist declined, but the man kept after him.

Finally the performer said, "You really do believe in me, don't you?"

"Oh, I do," the man assured him.

"OK," Zumbrati replied. "Get in the wheelbarrow."

So it is with belief; it demands that you get in the wheelbarrow. Set aside the concerns, lethargies, doubts, criticisms, hazy hopes, and loose-knit goals; climb into the wheelbarrow and ride the narrow wire in the high winds over the eerie chasms far below.

If you do, you might be alone, but you'll like yourself immensely for doing it. And it's then that you'll discover the magnificent meaning of these words proclaimed by William James, the dean of America's psychologists: "These, then, are my last words to you: Be not afraid of life. Believe that life *is* worth living and your belief will help create the fact."

10

How to Attract Wealth

I know a little Irishman named Pat who owns a file cabinet full of investments. He keeps on adding to them because he can't give up the habits that brought him his wealth.

When I first knew Pat, he had holes in his shoes and was struggling to find two nickels to rub together. Gradually he became aware of certain principles for becoming wealthy. He put them into practice. He never stopped doing those things that brought him financial abundance.

Pat was no different from the majority of those who attain wealth. It is not education, intelligence, personality, or special ability that attracts prosperity. It is the application of certain abundance principles.

They are not secrets. They are waiting to be applied by any ambitious person. Study the success patterns of the rich and you will find that most of them were patterned on these fundamentals:

1. *Use your mental money magnet.*
Know that becoming wealthy starts in your mind. Your mind will attract whatever it thinks about. Your mind gives energy to any condition, opportunity, or circumstance.

People worry about money. So they attract a scarcity to

worry about. Develop a prosperity consciousness. Let your mind dwell on the unlimited good and abundance of the universe. Be grateful for what you have and the unseen possibilities of the future. What you praise and are grateful for will infallibly multiply.

If you hang on to negative thoughts about scarcity and limitation, you will attract those conditions. You have been exposed to those all of your life. "Buy now!" "Save!" "Limited Supply!" These are typical of the propaganda to which you have been subjected.

You develop fears of not having enough money to get the things you want out of life. You end up creating the conditions that you fear most.

Replace fear with faith. Visualize all of the wonderful events and possessions that you want. Empower your mind with strong, positive thoughts that will attract prosperity rather than poverty.

I know a fellow who went into bankruptcy, then bounced back and today is wealthy.

"Although losing everything was tough to face," he said, "I never lost hope. Being without money was a circumstance. Being poor is a state of mind. I never allowed myself to think that way."

2. Understand the meaning of money.

Money is merely an exchange of services. The only things you can buy with money are the services of other people. You acquire money by rendering service. People exchanging services—that's how money is generated.

This means that the more service you generate, the more service will be available to you. People will construct a home for you, educate your children, furnish you with adventurous trips, and provide you with a luxurious automobile in response to service you render to others.

It's a marvelous system. People try to circumvent it or make it easy. It can't be done. The service (money) you receive will be in direct proportion to what you give.

3. *Decide what you are going to give.*
Most lessons of life are learned at an early age. I was fortunate. I grew up when times were hard. My parents did not give me money. I had to learn how to earn it.

When I was thirteen, I took over a paper route that no one wanted. It was in the poorest section of town; the people were mostly day laborers who were always scratching for some work to keep food on the table. They did not subscribe to papers or, if they did, would not have money to pay the delivery boy.

I built up the route and never lost a dime from a customer. But I made more callbacks than had ever been made. I found out when my customers were working and when they got their paychecks. That's the day that I called on them for payment.

I gave them more service than they expected. The Schmidts, for instance, lived a mile out of town on a dirt road that was usually not plowed in the winter. I left my bike on the main road and walked the mile to deliver their paper. I did that every day for a profit of about $.10 a week.

I did not think much about time, work, or how much money I made on each call. My goal was to get as many customers like the Schmidts as I possibly could. I learned that people appreciate service. If you are constantly looking for ways to give it, you will get it back in the form of money.

That was a valuable lesson for me. Little did I realize at the time how important it is to have faith in that principle. For in every job, industry, or company that I would have any contact with in the future, people would be standing in line waiting to convince me that there was no money to be made in that business.

If there was ever a shackle keeping the human mind from financial freedom, it is the statement "You can't make a living doing this." Don't *ever* let that fallacy invade your consciousness if you are seeking prosperity. It is not true. There is abundance and potential prosperity in toothpicks and bridges, hand soaps and wastepaper. Fortunes have been made in any activity that fills the needs of people, whether it means working with your hands or your heart and mind.

People who claim that you can't make a living at a particular activity are really saying that they don't want to do the things they have to do to make money. That is giving service. For the salesperson that means serving the customer and making a lot of daily calls. For the office worker that means looking about for all the things that need to be done and taking on tasks that perhaps others don't want.

If your goal is prosperity and abundance, decide what and how much service you will give. There is a price to pay for wealth. That price is service to others. Pack your days with serving others from early until late, and good fortune will assuredly come your way.

On the other hand, if you choose to complain, criticize, and blame circumstances for your lack, you will inevitably experience poverty and limitation. It starts with a state of mind.

4. *Try giving yourself away.*
Each person has a uniqueness that can grow into an exclusive niche in another's life. That uniqueness, it seems, is most highly prized when it is given away. There can, however, be no thought of being paid in any form, such as through a return of favors or special treatment.

This philosophy was neatly captured in a little book entitled *Try Giving Yourself Away.* The author, David Dunn, gave an idea to the New York Central Railroad that was used on its advertising calendar in 1924. The only reward was seeing his brainchild come to life wherever he went.

He tried giving away his thoughts and ideas in other ways and always found a glow of pleasure, "a happier way of living which all so earnestly seek and so few seem to find."

His story was printed first by *Forbes,* then in *Reader's Digest,* and finally put into book form in 1947 with reprints into the sixties, and it still may be available today.

The philosophy is simple. Let no charitable urge go unexpressed. Share with others your kindness, thoughtfulness, and ideas—not your money but the little deeds that cost nothing and benefit others in some way. Expect nothing in return, not even a response.

Dunn tells of a lot of his own experiences: sending a picture, poem, or cartoon that would interest a friend; buying a couple of youngsters who were standing hungrily in front of the popcorn wagon some bags of hot buttered popcorn; writing letters to those who had given him attentive service; phoning people to pay them compliments. Giving of himself became a style of thought and action that, he discovered, added a significant richness to his life.

It has been said many times in many ways, hasn't it? Cast your bread upon the waters! But it works. There are many people who practice living this way. They are folks who, when asked to do a favor, will say yes before they find out what it is. They don't wait to be asked, however. Their thoughts are always reaching out to add pleasantness to the lives of others.

Why do they do it? It might be because their own lives become so full that they can't possibly use all the wealth, love, success, and happiness that come to them.

In the marketplace these people never lose customers, usually having more than they can handle. They succeed not because their aspirations and attitudes are equated in dollars and cents but because of the heartfelt urge to answer the needs of others.

Their relationships run deeper by the day. Love, by its nature, grows. And who can deny affection to one whose deeds are designed to please others?

But most important, these people hold in high esteem the ones with whom they must live their lives: themselves! Of all the suggested prescriptions for wealth and happiness that is the single most powerful. You must like yourself. And when you do a kind act unselfishly for another, you can go to bed that night at peace with yourself.

Try giving yourself away! It's sound advice for successful living and attracting wealth.

5. *Start right where you are.*
You don't have to leave your job, start a company, win a lottery, or invent a new can opener to attract abundance. Start using these success principles right where you are. They will guide you in the direction of prosperity.

You might say "The boss is just sweating out retirement. The company is in miserable shape, hasn't grown in fifty years, and there is no future here."

Oh, yes, there is! The future is in the consciousness of the individual. The more problems there are in the company, the greater the opportunity for the positive optimism of the individual. Opportunity always comes dressed as hopelessness and a tangled mess of problems. Put all your energy, sinew, and creativity into solving problems and filling the needs of others. That's how the rich and successful achieved their fortunes. They perceived every difficulty and discordant situation as a possibility.

They went on to tackle the challenges of life with sweat and hope rather than run from them in despair and self-pity.

6. *Be the best that you can be.*
The wealthy people I have known just do what they do better than most others. They learn more, work harder, are more enthused, and stay focused more intensely than others doing the same thing.

A friend, Kibby, was a schoolteacher who started selling real estate part-time. He studied the market, ground development, and real estate trends. He was soon masterminding large developments of office buildings and residential communities.

Another friend, Dan, was selling automotive products out of a small storefront. He was enthused about his products, the customers, and the future. The little company has grown and Dan with it. He ended up heading the organization as it grew from mergers and acquisitions.

Dan loved what he did and did it as well as he could.

Are you doing your job as well as you know how to do it? Is there more that you can learn? Can you become more skillful, better informed, more creative?

Successful people have become so capable at what they do that they attract the attention of others. Others want to become associated with them in their progress.

And that leads us to the next principle for becoming wealthy.

7. *Magnify your efforts through others.*
There is a strategy of investment by which investors control a large asset with a small amount of money. It is named *leverage*.

You can use the same tactic with human effort. You can influence the efforts of a large number of people through a relatively small amount of your own effort. This is, by far, the method used most by the wealthy to acquire their abundance.

They have discovered how to extend and magnify their efforts through others. That means more service to others. And remember, more service means that more money is generated.

This principle is the dream of many. Start a little business of your own. Work hard; give good service. Then attract to your business others who want to be associated with success. Today entire industries are founded on this principle. The franchising business is one by which individuals have magnified or shared their success with others.

8. *Be patient.*
There are those who strike it rich overnight. They are scarce. Still, that seems to be the aspiration of many. So they go chasing rainbows, seeking the pot of gold. They are addicted to the "get rich quick" syndrome. The years slip by as the lottery tickets and fairy dust schemes pile up.

The majority who make it big do it gradually, a day at a time. They enjoy practicing the principles discussed here to such an extent that they become oblivious to wealth. It just evolves out of a life filled with a prosperity consciousness and a strong will to serve. These people seem to have an inborn desire to leave the world a little bit better than they found it.

Wealth acquired using these fundamentals is well earned. There is no better time or place to put them to use than right where you are right at this time. That's the joy and opportunity of being free.

11

Use Your Idea Power

Look about you. All that you see and touch and feel started as an idea in one person's mind.

Whether you are eating or sleeping or playing or working, you are submerged in the wonder of ideas. All of them were born, at one time, as a single revelation in a human brain.

All of the miracles of the future are waiting right now to be created as ideas in human thought.

Examine the lives of people who have become wealthy or successful in the world of business, and you will discover it was their ideas that lifted them from mediocrity. Their creations were often so obvious they may have escaped significance. But then who would have thought that fortunes were to be made from a paper clip, a better wrench, or a plan for selling cosmetics?

The human imagination is the greatest untapped resource in the world. What is true of the masses is also true of the individual. Ideas, seeded and nourished, can shape abundance and distinction for any who invest the efforts.

Indeed, creativity requires effort. That is why so many use their imaginations for little other than worry and fear. They exist day after day, governed by habit and routine, hoping the future will turn out well. They go to others to solve their problems and think their ideas.

Discover Your Aladdin's Lamp

Those hungering for success in their lives should be like Scheherazade in the *Arabian Nights*. King Schahriah married one wife after another simply to cut off their heads. Scheherazade was forced to become his wife. She then captured his fancy by telling a different story each night for 1,001 nights. He kept postponing her killing to see what the next story was going to be.

After three years she won the king's love and kingdom!

Among her stories was "Aladdin and the Wonderful Lamp." It was a legacy left for all. For each person has such a lamp. It is the gift of creativity. You have it within you. It is so powerful and limitless that its wonder is almost beyond comprehension. Perhaps that is why so few utilize even a fraction of this dynamic potential.

Ideas and ideas alone can separate you from the many. Others can work hard, use the same methods, acquire experience, and gain knowledge. But they do not have your individual gift to create.

You Have Creativity

You may feel you are not a creative person. That is not true. All people have creative ability.

Education is no factor in creative talent—except at times to suppress creativity. One survey showed that the more education people have, the less likely they are to be inventive.

Past training has little effect on creativity. The telegraph was worked out by Samuel Morse, a professional portrait painter. Robert Fulton, an artist, invented the steamboat. One of the great composers of American music, Irving Berlin, was a waiter who never learned to play the piano, except by ear and in F sharp.

Creativity has little relation to age. Alexander the Great conquered Persia at the age of twenty-five and was a creative genius in many nonmilitary ways as well. Grandma Moses started painting when she was seventy. Benjamin Franklin was at his creative best when he was past eighty. George Bernard Shaw won a Nobel Prize when he was seventy. He was still going strong in his nineties.

That force of motivation seems to be the fountain from which creativity flows. For ideas do not occur by accident or impulse. They grow from a deliberate quest planted in the mind and then fueled by effort.

Creativity Nourishes

Creating seems to strengthen and prolong life. The Federal Council on the Aging reports that people who are motivated to create live longer.

Years ago a man left a city to spend his last days in the desert. Having been diagnosed as terminally ill, he was content to settle into a barren shack on the fringe of a settled community.

Driven by an instinct unlike that of the dying, he sought hardship rather than comfort. Every day he trudged several miles up and down sandy slopes, lugging his water supply.

The survival impulses were unleashed on his hutlike home. Day-long efforts were turned into cupboards, latches, innovations, and finally added rooms.

Uninhibited by architectural restraints, this recluse lived years longer, creating what was finally a gobbledy-gook castle of crannies, nooks, sanctuaries, and devices of his own contrivance.

Here was an extended life reborn and nourished by creativity. Obsessed not by death but by life, this desert hermit put new shapes and forms into being. What greater meaning can be expressed by a soul's existence? That may very well be the purpose of life itself!

Creativity certainly sustains life. Novelist Carson

McCullers endured three strokes before she was twenty-nine. Crippled, in constant pain, and partially paralyzed, she suffered the saddening shock of a husband's suicide.

Others may have surrendered to such afflictions, but not Carson. Bolstered by her creative inspiration, she settled for writing no less than a page a day. On that schedule she turned out such distinguished novels as *The Member of the Wedding, The Ballad of the Sad Café, Reflections in a Golden Eye,* and *The Heart Is a Lonely Hunter.*

She died at the age of fifty and was eulogized by the *Saturday Review.* The article noted: "Carson was one of two or three best southern writers. If bad luck restricted her work, that was just bad luck. She was a very great artist and human being."

One of the most exuberant individuals I have known is an advertising executive whose every day was freshened by ideas, new concepts, and the design of marketing strategies. Although he was shoved out of the agency portals at age seventy, his years have continued to be founded in imaginative endeavors.

Recently he told me, "I bought a computer. I'm having more fun designing programs and feeding them into that little machine. Yesterday I started out at seven in the morning and was still going strong in the evening!"

How to Create

Creativity is a process more than a revelation.

Your mind is a massive, dormant giant in hibernation. It can perform its potential miracles for you only if commanded!

Do you know the trigger that motivates the mind to create action? *A question!* It is that simple!

A question opens the door to a channel of thought!

All directed thinking with a creative objective starts with a question. This is a "mind motivator."

Picture your mind as an intricate computer with unlimited power. It will respond only when you feed it a question.

If you are like most people, you may be spending a lot of time looking *outside* when your simplest and most productive sources of help rest *inside*—within yourself. And these untapped resources are waiting to be unlocked through mind motivators.

Every great accomplishment of humanity started in the mind of one person with a question.

For example, George Washington Carver devoted his entire life to answering just one question: "What is a peanut?" This one question motivated his mind to the benefit of all civilization.

This was the method used by the great Greek philosophers to probe the infinite wisdom of their minds—mind motivators. They stirred their thinking toward objectives by questioning themselves.

Knotty engineering problems have been overcome, million-dollar advertising programs have been conceived, administrative bottlenecks have been cleared just by using this technique—using a question to motivate the minds of a group.

I asked a friend of mine, an inventor, how he was different from other people. He said, "I ask myself questions. Each one of my inventions and patents is a result of asking myself a question. The first question usually is 'How can I lick this problem?' "

Problems Are Opportunities

Feeding a question to your imagination is more productive than pushing the keys on a computer. You will inevitably get a variety of possibilities. They will continue to flow if you continue to keep an open mind.

The question can be in the form of problems. That is why problems are opportunities. They stimulate creativity. Most of what is known today as progress started first as a problem and was transformed into an idea.

Do you have problems or limitations? Program them into your imagination. Hold them there. Don't let them go until they burst into possibilities. Then write them down and put them to work. The more you practice this, the better you will become.

Creativity is like any other developed talent. You use it or lose it. What a precious gift it is to use, this Aladdin's lamp, that can truly light up your life!

Help Others Be Creative

Helping people the most can often mean helping them identify or strengthen inner wants. In doing this, there is far more to be gained by asking the right questions than by knowing the right answers.

Telling all that you know will quickly cool the warmth of wants in another. Although you know beyond a sliver of doubt exactly how another should do a job or live a life, imposing your thoughts on someone will surely suppress that person's own wants.

So, how to unite with another to unveil those unseen wants? Questions are best. "How do you feel about that?" "What is your reaction to this?" "What is it that you really want to do? Have you decided that?" "What are the things that are most important to you in life?" "What do you want to achieve?"

It is often amazing how people begin to clarify their wants and directions if given the opportunity just to talk loosely and spontaneously about themselves. There are many who have never allowed themselves to want much beyond what they have. They don't believe it is possible.

Rather than open their minds and hearts to new desires and dreams of wondrous chunks of life, they reconcile their hopes to only what they have. The exciting, adventurous, abundant lives of the few represent a party to which most see themselves uninvited.

Through your questions and suggestions you can become the host who is inviting others to stir some of those dormant aspirations and wants.

Ask "Why?"

When another person starts thinking and talking in reaction to your questions, a remarkable little want definer is the single word *why*.

"Why do you want to be a manager?" "Why do you want a trip around the world?" "Why do you want to be the best parent who ever existed?" "Why do you want to work at something else?"

Those *why*s can unclutter some tangled inclinations. When a person can put into words exactly why something is wanted, it can be like a light turned on in a darkened room.

There is the story of the fellow who trained a flea to jump on command.

Then, day by day, he pulled out one of the flea's legs. Every time a leg was removed, the insect had more difficulty jumping. When the last leg was finally gone, the fellow said, "Jump!" The flea, of course, couldn't move.

"This simply shows that when you remove all of a flea's legs, the flea becomes deaf," the guy explained.

A lot of people are trying to run their lives like that. They're picking out the wrong causes for the effects they see or would like to see in their lives.

A psychological study was done on people recovering from heart attacks. It was found that those who owned pets were less likely to have a recurrence than non-pet owners. The conclusion: that one who is recovering from a heart attack should get a cat or dog.

Completely overlooked were the qualities within people that made them want pets—patience, tenderness, concern for other life, and a need for some sort of companionship. Those are the same tendencies that aid healing.

Along the same vein were the studies done to tie coffee drinking to heart problems. They were started when some statistical evidence surfaced that those who drank more than five cups of coffee daily were susceptible to heart attacks.

After a bunch of money and time was spent, no definite correlation could be established. Little wonder.

Apparently it was never considered that the inclinations that caused excessive coffee drinking were the very same ones that ended up as funny pictures on cardiograms.

Think of the people you know who are coffee freaks. How many are heavy smokers, in hectic jobs, nervous, excessive eaters of the wrong foods, or prone to other addictions? Hmmmm. Remove a flea's legs, and it becomes deaf. . . .

The point of all this is one that's critical to your success. The people who make it big ask "Why?" until they come up with the right reasons.

They are the ones that are making use of their Aladdin's lamps!

Creativity Benefits

Few of life's activities generate the rich satisfaction that creativity provides. A profound sense of accomplishment, fulfillment, and self-expression arises when you arrange your world a bit differently.

Your efforts need not be exalted or towering to be joyful. Establishing a new customer, trying a new recipe, or composing a letter to a friend can be pleasantly rewarding.

Nor are you limited as to the place or time. You can stir yourself to creative activities right where you are in the hours at hand.

Like most of life's merry moments, creativity is experienced only through intent and practice. The benefits, however, far exceed the efforts.

To motivate yourself to create, you might keep in mind that in addition to a healthier, happier life you just might live longer!

12

Be in Control with Self-Talk

You were once thought to be mentally unhinged if you went about talking to yourself. Not anymore. It is now the acknowledged ritual for health and achievement. In fact it has become an art and a science in itself.

What is there to talking to yourself? Who is "yourself," and who is doing the talking? It seems there really are two of you. "Yourself" is one—the one who drives your car, ties shoelaces, types, monitors the millions of complex functions of the body, and can be taught all sorts of skills to enable you to enjoy life.

Then there is the other you. That's the Boss. Boss is the one doing the talking. And the talking usually consists of criticizing, bullyragging, warning, nagging, ridiculing, and agitating Yourself. In other words Boss is indeed a very poor boss. Boss keeps Yourself locked up, obstructed, and limited. The New Age psychology offers hope for changing that. Bosses are now being taught how to talk more kindly and supportively to Yourselves.

You Are Your Own Obstacle

Psychology Today described, for example, how Olympic

athletes are taught to stop those inner Bosses from saying
  "You don't belong here."
  "You can't possibly beat him."
  "She is much better than you are."
  At an Elite Athlete Camp on the campus of Arizona
State University, Olympic contenders are trained to re-
hearse their events mentally as winners rather than losers.
  Tim Gallwey, who has written several bestsellers about
the "inner game" of golf, tennis, and skiing, suggests:

> If human beings did not have a tendency to inter-
> fere with their own ability to perform and learn, there
> would be no Inner Game. But the fact is that because
> of self-interference, few of us perform up to the level
> of our potential for more than brief moments at a time.

How Are You Doing?

There need be no mystery about how well you are playing
the inner game. What are your scores in life? Are you
satisfied? Are others who have no more talent than you
doing much better? And are there inner voices like these?
  "You're not ready yet."
  "She won't like you."
  "You don't know enough."
  "It will never work for you."
  "They will think you're ridiculous."
  Of more serious consequence physically is the badger-
ing little inner Boss who harps at Yourself like this:
  "Hurry! Hurry! Hurry!"
  "You can't stand any more of this."
  "You'll never have time to get everything done."
  "What if? What if? What if?"
  "Watch out! You'll get sick!"
  As the taunting rises, so does the anxiety, tension, and
blood pressure.

Be Your Own Booster

I recently played in a two-day golf tournament. I had the unique experience of playing with the person who finished first and the one who finished last. The one who finished first did not have the natural ability to play as well as the other.

There was, however, a significant difference in the way they treated themselves. The tail-ender berated himself with remarks such as these after every bad shot:

"You dummy! What's wrong with you?"

"You must have left your brains in the parking lot."

The winner, on the other hand, got so excited about his good shots that he forgot about the bad ones. All his remarks centered around how great he was playing and how he visualized winning the trophy.

Life is like that. It might be viewed as a game. You are both the spectator and the participant. Are you going to do better viewing yourself as a winner or a loser? What will bring out the best in you? Boos or applause?

There are those who would never think of treating an employee or another person the way they treat themselves. Why not be as good to Yourself as you would be to others?

Be Good to Yourself

A new era of human awareness has dawned radiant with hope and wonder! Encased within your being is the most miraculous mechanism in the universe, explosive with unknown miracles. Yourself is pleading for a Boss who will help rather than hinder Yourself's joyful expression of life.

The inner Boss must praise, support, reinforce, respect, and genuinely like Yourself. Patience must be practiced while Yourself grows, learns, expands in wisdom, and becomes trained in new skills. Failure and discouragement should be diluted with rest and encouragement.

Every person who ever achieved anything in his or her

life had an invisible Boss who steadfastly believed in the unseen Self. Never giving up, staunchly dedicated to the marvel of Yourself, an inner voice like that will unfold all sorts of unventured vistas in your life.

Self-Talk Influences Relationships

Your attitudes and the inner script that evolve can have a profound effect on your relationships and health. The most common cause of mental anguish and physical distress is conflict with another.

It need not be serious. Perhaps a clerk in a store slights you. Soon you're inflamed about the disgusting performance of all servants to the public. Or your spouse pricks your ego with the thorn of a disagreeable remark. It finds its way into a warm, fertile spot in the mind that is cultured by self-pity. It does not take long for the mind to become a catalog of abuses you have endured since courtship due to the negligence of this one whose life should be committed to molding your delirious day-to-day happiness.

No further examples need be supplied. You've been there yourself a time or two, haven't you?

You Start Judging

The mind becomes the high court of all human behavior. You have been treated unfairly, and that's not fair! Well, it really isn't, and you don't care who knows it! In fact it becomes a "matter of principle," sticking up for what's right, defending yourself, and something should be done about it! And so . . .

You Attack

Now the mind becomes a battleground. It starts with minor skirmishes. You begin rehearsing what you will say to the person(s). But you know you will encounter resistance. So the joust intensifies. You say this, and the other person will say that, and then you respond to that, and then you get to whatever.

Those are the scripts that tumble about in the imagination. They may get no further than shaggy illusions. After all, actual confrontations can be even more curdled and frightening, can't they?

But in whatever form it takes, you're attacking the other person. You might reason that you're actually defending yourself, but reality would dictate that it is attacking.

This mental state may last for hours, days, or a lifetime, but it will, infallibly, instigate the next step.

You Get Sick

This might be as slight as fatigue, depression, headache, flu, or a cold or as harsh as ulcers, heart attack, or cancer.

The severity of the sickness is in direct relation to the length of time and intensity of conflict existing in the mind. Harbor and keep fueling those ill feelings for a prolonged period and they will dig into the body in a remarkably destructive manner.

Is that what you want? If it is not, then we can consider some suggestions that might help in diluting those negative attitudes.

You have become sick by picturing yourself as a victim being trampled and abused by others.

From there you judge and attack your adversaries, a routine that most assuredly is destructive to your physical condition.

The new science of biofeedback exposes the inner Bosses for what they are—tyrants that bedevil Yourselves into physical distress. Meters monitor biological processes such as heart rate, temperature, brain wave activity, blood pressure, and muscle tension. You can learn how to reshape the inner Boss to influence Yourself positively rather than negatively. Remarkable changes are experienced in physiological states to gain control over migraine headaches, hypertension, and other bodily miseries.

Stop Judging

Yes, if you can stop judging, do it. You've been told that before. From long ago came the advice "Judge not, that ye be not judged." Judgment leads to controversy and conflict.

Your mind believes it has to be right to survive. Always being right means making just about everybody else wrong in some way. That can lead to a few trash cans of aggravations, grinding stomachs, and wrenched feelings. In fact the number-one source of all frustration and conflict is the opinion that other people are not acting the way we think they "should" act. That includes family, neighbors, friends, bosses, customers, strangers—even a wife or husband!

Peace, a quiet heart, and robust health will never abide with a mind that is judgmental. Situations and people must, at times, be evaluated, yes, but not judged. There is a difference between appraising the performance of people and making value judgments of right and wrong or good and bad.

Judgment is so useless. People's behavior is always rewarded or punished by circumstances, by their conscience, not judgment. Judgment is inevitably more damaging to the one judging than the one being judged.

Negative Self-Talk Develops

The human mind can become totally enraptured with the judgment game. It will drag you into this sport in a split-second reaction.

"Look at that idiot driver!"

"I didn't like the tone of her voice."

"He has no right to talk to me like that."

"Things are really messed up around here."

"Don't they care about the way I feel?"

"You're not going to push me around!"

Well, it sometimes goes on from the first smell of coffee until the evening news clobbers you with all sorts of atrocities. As the day unfolds, your mind is making judgment calls in all the observations and encounters with others.

People are right or wrong. Fair or unfair. Likable or unlikable. Too aggressive or too indifferent. Good or bad. Pleasant or unpleasant. For you or against you. Those against you may be just one or the whole world. So you have to stick up for yourself or "what's right." (Of course sticking up for yourself is always "what's right.") And that leads to attack. But first, let's deal with judgment.

Attacking Does Not Work

Such a critical perspective leads to hate, anger, depression, and attack. Attacking others, mentally or verbally, does not work. Ever! It never makes your life better. Why? Because it never makes anyone else's life better. And maybe sometimes that's the purpose of attack—to make someone else feel as tormented as you do. That's called *revenge.*

But that never works either. Revenge never made anyone's life better. Sadistically satisfying perhaps, but not better. An inner ire or indignation may be quieted for a time by unloading on the rude clerk or indifferent salesperson. But it never brings joy.

Try Forgiving

Joy blossoms only from love. Not necessarily the emotion of love, but the attitude of love. The attitude of love is simply the absence of judgment and attack. For most, that usually requires forgiving.

Forgiving is nothing more than the realization that people function from fear or love. Fear is the cry of the senseless ego being threatened and will lead to anger, pain, self-justification, and self-pity.

Would you add to the misery of others by judging, attacking, and causing them to defend their fear? If the answer is no, then that is forgiving.

If you find that your own mind refuses to withdraw

from the skirmish with another, then first forgive yourself. If you don't, you will inevitably hurt yourself. Your mind, stimulated by fear, judging, and attacking, will lead to some type of destruction.

Your productivity, effectiveness, or prosperity will erode. Or your feelings will become raw and afflicted. Those conditions, packaged and shelved in the human mind, will unfailingly lead to sickness.

The power of self-talk has become a major issue in the shaping of our lives. Look within yourself. Get to know that inner Boss and Yourself. How are they getting along?

Build that Boss into a positive force. You will then be in control of your performance, body, and relationships!

13

Get Pumped Up!

In 1622 the Spanish galleon *Atocha* was making her maiden voyage from Havana to Spain when she was struck by a hurricane. Swept over a barrier reef forty miles west of Florida, the *Atocha* sank with a cargo of gold and silver.

Hopelessly optimistic, 347 years later, Mel Fisher, a retired chicken farmer from California, went looking for the *Atocha*. Centuries of currents, tides, and shifting silt would have scattered and buried the treasure beneath miles of open sea.

Undaunted by the enormous odds against him, Fisher wrung out sixteen years of tedious searching for his pot of gold. Even the loss of a son and daughter-in-law by drowning did not stop him.

On Saturday, July 20, 1985, the quest ended. Beneath five feet of silt the watery grave of silver bars worth up to $400 million was discovered!

Mel Fisher may have uncovered more than buried treasure. His inexhaustible devotion to a dream will undoubtedly strengthen the hearts of many who are nurturing some lofty vision for their lives!

Persistence! Many have described it. Elbert Hubbard,

the turn-of-the-century author and publisher, wrote:

> The line between failure and success is so fine that we
> scarcely know when we pass it: so fine that we are
> often on the line and do not know it. How many peo-
> ple have thrown up their hands at a time when a little
> more effort, a little more patience, would have
> achieved success. As the tide goes out, so it comes in.
> In business, sometimes, prospects may seem darkest
> when really they are on the turn. A little more persis-
> tence, a little more effort, and what seemed hopeless
> failure may turn to glorious success. There is no failure
> except in no longer trying. There is no defeat except
> from within, no really insurmountable barrier save our
> own inherent weakness of purpose.

One idea stands out in that: "There is no failure except
in no longer trying." Those who are the champions of
achievement have learned to be immune from any of the
usual discouragements of failure.

Tom Watson, the golfer, was asked how he would feel
if he lost as he tried in 1983 for his fifth British Open title.
"I don't think much about that," he replied. "I've lost
before. But, then, I've won before, too. I learned to lose
before I learned to win."

Dealing with Adversity

Mel Fisher demonstrated how to handle losing and adversity. Put it behind you! Today is a new day! Every morning
he greeted his employees with the statement "Today's the
day!" Saturday, July 20, he was right!

History is sprinkled with the Fishers, those who perse-
vered. We know nothing of the hundreds of thousands who
gave up, stopping short of achieving their dreams. If Columbus had turned back after sixty-five days of sailing the
uncharted seas, no one would have blamed him. But then
no one would have remembered him either!

Ironweed, a novel, was a phenomenal bestseller and 1984 Pulitzer Prize winner. The author, William Kennedy, had written several manuscripts, all of them rejected by publishers, before his sudden success. *Ironweed* was rejected by thirteen publishers before finally being accepted for publication.

"The thought of not writing every day never occurred to me," said Kennedy. "Even if *Ironweed* had not been published I would have continued writing."

So he became wealthy with movie and publishing contracts and a vast public following.

The Kennedys and Fishers demonstrate more than rugged perseverance and dogged determination. Their inevitable discouragements seem to be subdued by a diamond-hard hope and unquenchable optimism. Their minds continue undisturbed by any notions of giving up.

Nothing Ventured, Nothing Gained

Those people who venture out and never give up have learned that failure may be unpleasant but not tragic. Indeed experiencing a setback can be of enormous meaning. For failure does for living what a prism does for sunshine! It breaks the substance of your life into separate qualities, allowing you to see each more clearly. That's growth. It's getting to know yourself better.

Today many people avoid a change in a career or a promising enterprise because of the chance of missing a few steak dinners or the monthly payment on the car. Besides that, "What would our friends think if we failed?"

In a country that is becoming increasingly success-oriented, many people are being held back, limited, by the humiliation of failure.

We must preserve our freedom to fail; without it lives become narrow channels with no exciting excursions to explore potentials and find out what we can become.

Let us try fresh ideas knowing full well they won't all work; but remember us for the ones that do rather than branding us dunderheads for the ones that don't.

Many people cringe at failures because they do not have a high enough opinion of themselves. The opinion you have of yourself relates directly to the amount of failure you can tolerate before you stop trying and stop achieving.

Why not look at failure differently? See your failures as stepping-stones to success. Realize that the more failures you have, the more successful you will become. You probably have heard of Ty Cobb, the immortal baseball star. For a number of years he held the record he set in 1915 of ninety-six stolen bases. But have you heard of Max Carey? In 1922 Carey stole fifty-one bases out of fifty-three attempts for an amazing 96 percent success ratio compared with Cobb's 70 percent based on ninety-six out of 134 attempts. Carey was cautious not to fail. And so he succeeded far less than Cobb. People are not remembered by how few times they fail but by how often they succeed.

You will never find out how successful you can be unless you repeatedly expose yourself to failure.

Try laughing at failures. Tomorrow, see how often you can fail. Then laugh it off. Discover that failure does not hurt; there is no pain involved. In fact it can be a learning experience, even humorous, if you learn to take it lightly.

Replace in your mind the disaster of failure with these words by Theodore Roosevelt: "Far better it is to dare mighty things, to win glorious triumphs, even though checkered by failure, than to take rank with those poor spirits who neither enjoy much nor suffer much, because they live in the gray twilight that knows not victory nor defeat."

Get Pumped Up!

Mel Fisher's declaration "Today's the day" was his way of making the most of each day. He kept himself pumped up.

Every day is like a lifetime. A new day is born; at night it will fade away, never to be lived again.

Why not make the most of each day? Live it with gusto!

You have the power to do that. But only you; it isn't the cloudy day, the dent in the fender, a grumpy spouse, or an aching back that determines your mood. It's you!

Manage your reactions and you can be in control of your life. Look for the possibilities in every problem or adversity. Be positive. Pump yourself up with enthusiasm. Learn to live with gusto! Nothing will bring you more of life's riches than approaching each day with this vigor and dedication!

If you are in the business of dealing with people, personal enthusiasm is the most powerful force you can develop to persuade or influence another.

The Power of Enthusiasm

It has been said that enthusiasm is the key to the achievement not only of great things but also of anything worthwhile.

> Enthusiasm is a wonderful word. But more, it is a wonderful feeling. It is a way of life. It is a magic spark that transforms "being" into "living." It makes hard work easy—and enjoyable. There is no better tonic for depression, no greater elixir for whatever happens to be wrong at the moment, than enthusiasm.
>
> No person who is enthusiastic about his or her work has anything to fear from life. All the opportunities in the world—and they are as plentiful today as ever, despite what some people say—are waiting to be grasped by the people who are in love with what they are doing.
>
> Enthusiasm for work and life is the most precious ingredient in any recipe for successful living. And the greatest feature of this ingredient is that it is available to all—within themselves!

Those are the thoughts of Samuel Goldwyn, the great American moviemaker. He was giving advice that has been passed down through the ages by those who have learned to make each day count.

Enthusiasm Is Important

Ralph Waldo Emerson wrote: "Nothing great was ever achieved without enthusiasm." That includes writing a letter, serving a customer, planting a flower bed, painting a picture, washing windows—in other words, making the most out of each of life's moments.

Enthusiasm is to a person what electricity is to a light, fuel to a car, or flame to a fireplace. Fire can't be made with dead embers. Nor can enthusiasm be stirred by spiritless people.

Enthusiasm must be nourished with new actions, new aspirations, new efforts, and new vision. It must be fed until it becomes a part of each of the day's activities, a way of living.

It isn't until enthusiasm becomes ingrained by intent and habit that one becomes an "enthusiastic person."

Form the Habit

Form the habit of being enthusiastic! That's the secret of squeezing the joy out of each moment in time.

A wise old teacher, walking in the woods with a boy, stopped by a small plant just breaking through the ground. Next to it was a fair-sized stem loosely rooted in the soft mulch. Next to that were a shrub and a tree.

The man asked the boy to pull each one out. The lad easily pulled out the stem and the tiny plant. But he tugged and tugged at the shrub and, of course, said it was impossible to uproot the tree.

Then the sage said, "So it is with our habits. When first formed they are not deeply rooted in our consciousness and can be pulled out quite easily. But when allowed to grow and age, they become so deeply rooted it is quite impossible to remove them."

By habit, enthusiasm for life can be as deeply implanted in your spirit as a giant oak.

Every second of life is like a musical note. Shape each one with enthusiasm, and soon there is a melodic chord. These become habits that make each day a song.

Beethoven said it best:

"From the glow of enthusiasm I let the melody escape. I pursue it. It flies again, it disappears, it plunges into a chaos of diverse emotions. I catch it again, I seize it, I embrace it with delight. . . . I multiply it by modulations, and at last I triumph in the first theme. There is the whole symphony."

Enthusiasm is both an attitude and an emotion. It starts with an attitude about something. That can be shining shoes, chatting with a friend, selling a new product, or living the next hour.

From a thought it must then be transformed into action. The creed of the sales world, "To be enthusiastic you must act enthusiastic!" is based on psychological fact.

You cannot sit passively and wish your way into feeling joy, happiness, or enthusiasm. You must act out those emotions to feel them.

You will discover that there is nothing more contagious and persuasive than enthusiasm. And, yes, lovable! Aren't enthusiastic people the ones who are easiest to like and love and be with?

Perhaps that is why it has been said that *enthusiasm* is the most beautiful word on Earth.

Look at your life with fresh vision and a sense of adventure! There have to be ponies out there that perhaps you have overlooked. Start your days by saying to yourself what Mel Fisher said: "Today's the day!"

Out there in the sea of opportunities and possibilities rest unlimited buried treasures for those who just don't know how to give up!

14

Stop Holding Yourself Back

"The only thing we have to fear is fear itself."

Words like those were the artistry of the Franklin Roosevelt speeches that lifted a nation's spirit when it had been frayed by depression and war.

What could have been his greatest oration, however, was never delivered. It was to be a Jefferson Day address on April 13, 1945. President Roosevelt had recently returned from Yalta and a conference with Stalin and Churchill. Plans were seeded for the Allied victory and the international gathering in San Francisco to draw up the charter for the United Nations.

Wednesday evening, April 11, Roosevelt finalized his draft of the Jefferson Day address.

The next day, the president was going over some official papers when he slumped forward, unconscious, at his desk. The rich, melodic voice was silenced forever.

If he had lived to speak the next day, the nation would have heard that doubts and fears must be conquered, the science of human relationships must be cultivated, and hope must be preserved for a peaceful, happier life for all people throughout the world.

These would have been his closing words: "The only

limit to our realization of tomorrow will be our doubts of today."

How unfortunate that the sentence was not flung out to be better known. For it certainly would have remained to be quoted as an answer to the question that hovers in just about everyone's mind: "What's holding me back?"

The only limit to the realization of tomorrow's dreams are the doubts hung on to today. That's what's holding you back! You! You want to do so many things, to be and to grow into the fullest possible expressions of your life. Still, you are afraid to let go of what you are and have.

In the ancient Chinese book of wisdom, *I Ching,* is the quotation "All the suffering of mankind is produced by attachment to a previous condition of existence."

If you continue to cling to what you are today and still long to be something else tomorrow, there is conflict. This disharmony is translated into your body and human conditions. You look at your life and ask, "What is the meaning of this? Why is this happening to me?"

If you are to grow into a full "realization of tomorrow," agree to be someone else. If not, you are like a babe in the womb who refuses to be born or a chick who won't break the shell to emerge into a strange new world.

Be willing to die continuously to be born. That's as true in achieving new heights in selling goods and services as it is in becoming a better spouse or parent.

What are the doubts that limit our realization of tomorrow, the attachment to a previous condition that causes suffering? It could be the way you see yourself. You picture yourself trapped in a job, a set of responsibilities, limitations, obligations, and problems from which there is no escape, no freedom. Realize that all the conditions you view as narrowing are the very doorways by which you can become free.

Look for Ponies

In all the ways you hold yourself back, there are ponies if you look deeply enough.

The customers who turn you down, the promotions that you don't get, and the hoped-for success that appears so elusive are all spawning beds for personal growth and learning.

From the problems of those you love that fall as burdens on your heart come the opportunities to give, help, and understand.

From your loneliness and despair comes the challenge of looking within and discovering new veins of character, richer emotions, and alternative interests.

From those who criticize, ignore, and mistreat you comes the ability to rise above self-pity and gain new strongholds of self-sufficiency.

Because of the love and appreciation you sometimes sense you lack, you can acquire the capacity to love without being loved.

That, in itself, can be quite a pony!

Examine Your Beliefs

You perceive the world not the way it is but the way you are. From all that you have been, you build your reality. It is unique. It is one of a kind. There are no two human beings whose realities are identical. Most important, your reality shapes your behavior. To that reality, then, you become a master or a servant.

Unfortunately, most are servants. This is because realities are molded by the past, not the future. And people are inclined to become imprisoned rather than empowered by their past.

Beliefs, for example, tend to free or limit. There are the spiritual beliefs and values that are the cherished guidelines that enrich your life. On the other hand, there are false beliefs that are bagged and preserved from early childhood. These are guarded tenaciously; people will struggle and despair to justify worn-out beliefs.

Beliefs that you are limited, that you must experience sickness, that age will deprive you of vigor and vitality, that to dream is futile are false beliefs that hold you back.

Then there are the beliefs in barriers, that there are no possibilities within reach. Instead of shaking these from their realities, many waited for history to do that. Here are some real classics:

- "TV won't be able to hold on to any market it captures after the first six months. People will soon get tired of staring at a plywood box every night."—Darryl F. Zanuck, head of 20th Century-Fox, in 1946
- "With over 50 foreign cars already on sale here, the Japanese auto industry isn't likely to carve out a big slice of the U.S. market for itself."—*Business Week* in 1958
- "Sensible and responsible women do not want to vote."—Grover Cleveland, 1905
- "Who wants to hear actors TALK?"—Harry M. Warner, Warner Bros., 1927
- "I think there's a world market for about five computers."—Thomas J. Watson, IBM chairman, in 1943
- "There is no likelihood man can ever tap the power of the atom."—Robert Millikan, Nobel Prize in physics, 1923

Aside from your beliefs, what old habits have shackled you and held you back? Days tend to be lived in the same way. Little habits become entrenched routines. The same food is eaten in the same way at the same place. Relationships become dreary when those involved talk of the same things in the same way.

Some habits are destructive. Those that impair health are often viewed as impossible to surrender. Habits of thought can make us cynical, hopeless, fearful, and bitter. It is easier to be critical than to be correct.

Got Any Dead Rosebushes?

In Russia many years ago a czar came upon a sentry standing at attention in a secluded spot in the palace garden. He asked the man, "Sentry, what are you guarding?"

"I don't know, sire," the guard replied. "I was ordered to my post by the captain of the guard."

Calling the captain of the guard, the czar questioned him concerning the sentry's post. The captain could give no better answer than "Regulations call for a sentry at that particular spot."

Determined to find the reason for this apparently useless provision, the czar ordered the archives to be searched to determine the origin of the regulation. Finally it was learned that many years before, Catherine the Great had planted a rosebush there and ordered a sentry placed beside it to keep it from being trampled. The rosebush had been dead for more than one hundred years, but the sentry was still there.

Why Spend Time Guarding Useless Old Habits?

How many things do people spend a lot of time guarding that long ago stopped serving any useful purpose in their lives? A whole batch of them come under the heading of "negative attitudes." It has been found that these are protected even more vigorously than positive thoughts.

Greed and selfishness are good examples. These characteristics are useful to small children as they learn to stick up for themselves and become concerned about their possessions. These traits can also be the seeds of ambition, pride, self-acceptance, and a healthy desire to get ahead. On the other hand, as greed and selfishness are preserved into adulthood, they can lead to loneliness and criticism.

P. D. Armour, the meat packer, had an appropriate comment about these traits. Years ago he offered to buy

each of his employees a new suit of clothes, expecting a
certain sense of moderation in their purchases. One fellow,
however, went out and bought the most extravagant set of
evening clothes he could find. When Armour got the bill,
he called the fellow into his office to make sure the suit
was actually that expensive. When told the amount was
correct, Armour said it would be paid but remarked, "I
have packed a great many hogs in my time but this is the
first time that I ever dressed one!"

Be a giver rather than thinking only of getting!

Pursue Useful Purposes
and Look Toward the Future!

The point is that you can become obsolete over the years
sheltering old habits and characteristics that should have
been discarded years ago. They become like chains holding you back, draining valuable time and energy that could
be spent pursuing useful purposes. Living, to be exciting,
must be done in the future. You cannot look backward and
forward at the same time. Only by ceasing to spend time as
a custodian of the rosebushes of the past can you dream of
the future.

Accept Responsibility for Change

The story is told about a fellow in New York whose life was
bungling along rather miserably when he decided to consult a psychiatrist to help him change. He selected an
address on Park Avenue and entered the doctor's reception
room, tastefully appointed but without a receptionist.
There were two doors, one marked "Men" and the other
"Women."

He went through the door marked "Men" and came
upon two other doors, one marked "Extrovert" and the
other "Introvert." Knowing he was an introvert, he opened
that door and found himself in a room with two more

doors. One read "Those Making at Least $20,000" and the other "Those Making Less than $20,000."

He knew he made less than that sum, so he entered that door—and found himself back on Park Avenue!

The man learned something about the habitual barriers to change that for most are painful to learn.

Reluctant to change, the man was like most people who blame their agonies on others. They can be characterized by an incident when a mother heard a caterwauling commotion from another room.

"Tommy!" she cried. "Stop pulling the cat's tail!"

"I ain't pullin' the cat's tail," Tommy called back. "I'm just standin' on it. It's the cat that's doin' the pullin'!"

"It's not my fault!" people are saying. "It's everybody else that's causing my troubles!" So their lives don't change. They remain locked up or back on Park Avenue where they came from.

That's a sober reminder that you are accountable for your life. You're responsible for what you are, where you're going, what you'll be. Your happiness, success, peace, and well-being result from *your* decisions, not those of others.

If you seem to be held back or have an unfair share of miseries, quite naturally you wish that the world would change. "If the person I'm living with would only communicate or appreciate me or understand me or be more romantic or . . . or. . . ."

"If the company would pay me more or give me a chance or change so I could. . . ." Those are small parts of the laments of the many who are hanging on to what they are, resisting self-change.

Before your life will change, you must change. Accept that; trust it. Know that no matter what the size of your problems or pain or hopelessness, the misery is merely an illusion held in the mind. It will vanish into its nothingness if you become determined to change.

Just make the decision to change. Don't worry about how. A teacher will always appear to show you the way if you become firm in your determination.

Get Out of Donner Pass!

In October 1846, a group of eighty-seven people going to California became trapped by snow. Known as the Donner Party, named for its two Donner families, their fate in the Sierra Nevada is remembered as Donner Pass.

Sealed in the pass by heavy snow, they soon exhausted their supplies. After forty days, half the group had died of starvation and sickness.

Then two of the men set out to the nearest village. It was, they found, within walking distance. They made it easily and returned with a rescue party to lead the survivors to safety.

Why did they wait forty days, facing starvation and death, to leave the site? Why didn't someone venture out before then? It was because they did not want to leave their possessions behind. They grew weak and exhausted attempting to get their wagons and supplies out of the snow-blocked canyon.

Before you judge those settlers too harshly, imagine for a moment that you could be mired in your own Donner Pass. You might be dragging a load of baggage that has your life in a rut. You seem to be going nowhere, but you see no way out.

The further along in life you go, the more baggage and burdens you accumulate. Possessions, obligations, relationships, *shoulds*, *ought to*s, habits, finances, and routines keep piling up. You lose control; each day it is a strain to haul the heavy loads along.

You have the feeling that you must get away from it all. The world is closing in on you, and there's no way out. You tell yourself that there has got to be more to life than what you're experiencing.

There is! And you can create it! You have been empowered to get far more from life than what you have now. You begin by getting out of your Donner Pass.

Perhaps getting out may be as simple as resolving to walk away. Be willing to let go of the past, get in charge of your life, and free yourself to create your future.

Are People Holding You Back?

What people are holding you in bondage? Whom are you trying to impress? For those you feel you must please are holding you captive.

The opposite is also true. Are you standing guard over anyone who must act or feel in accordance with your judgment? If so, you're being bound. For the guard is really the prisoner.

The past adds untold burdens of possessions. Possessions become addictions. What you must possess possesses you. The futility of this situation will someday become apparent.

A friend recently cleaned out the old family home. It was an ancient two-story house of four bedrooms and spacious attic.

"Mother had been rattling around in that place for years," my friend related. "Then she passed on. We hauled out carloads of stuff she had been accumulating. It opened my eyes, though. When we got through, I did the same thing at my own home. I tossed out things that were only ways of hanging on to the past."

What *ought to*s and *should*s are you carrying around from the past? What old battles are you still fighting? What old injustices are you still harboring that rob you of peace and joy? What could you set aside by simply forgiving and forgetting?

Many people are going to seminars and reading books trying to discover who they are. Why worry? Why not invent the person you want to be? The best way to predict the future is to create it.

Open your mind. Set aside the past and the thoughts that repress. Seek out new ideas, fresh possibilities, and unwilted dreams. Nourish your life with a reality built with newborn truths.

15

Dealing with Stress

The concussion of a clanging alarm clock is jostling your sleep-drenched mind. "Uhhh—I'll give my Christmas bonus for just another ten minutes," you think. But, no. There's a meeting, and this is Thursday. Gobs of debris must be cleared out before the weekend. Coffee will help. Three cups later you find it does. The pulse is quicker. The brain is clear. All systems are on go.

Except the traffic. Road repairs have imprisoned you in a line of cars sentencing you to a minimum fifteen-minute delay. "I should have gone the other way. Is it too late? Can I hit the shoulder and pass the cars ahead? What are they holding things up for? They can let those cars get around that grader! What will the others think when I drag in fifteen minutes late?" Frantic thoughts turn on more adrenaline.

The meeting doesn't do anything to slow things down. In between nips of coffee you try to bat down some of the resistance to your viewpoint. Not enough time.

Problems Keep Coming

The get-together breaks up. But not the pattern of activity. More coffee. More problems. More rush. More traffic. The stomach feels like a clenched fist. Sweaty palms, throbbing head, and frustration are all clamoring for a tranquilizer and a quiet evening of TV.

But there are just a couple of little decisions that must be made before dinner. Like where will we spend next year's vacation? And Alfred has a learning problem, so shall we move him to a special school? And Jennifer must have braces whether she likes it or not.

There is no longer any appetite or hope for a peaceful evening. Simple anxiety and tension have been replaced by a kind of smoldering rage. The inner mechanism is in full battle posture, ready to defend you against the world, its people, and the pits into which you have been thrust. You are experiencing the bubonic plague of the twentieth century—stress.

Dangers of Stress

Forget about cholesterol, asbestos fibers, sugar, and air clogged with carbon monoxide. The number-one killer today is stress. Endured over a period of time, this hoarded pressure must find a release. Ulcers, nervous breakdowns, heart attacks, high blood pressure, and even cancer are a few of the outlets the body finds. Or relief could be sought in behavior—compulsive eating, temper tantrums, and addictions. These could all be triggered by stress.

Researchers in the areas of religion, science, and human behavior are targeting stress. What is being discovered is little more than your common sense tells you but you don't want to admit.

Gremlins of Stress

You cause your own stress. Now, that's hard to digest along with your Valium. It's that cockeyed boss, stains on the carpeting, screaming kids, weeds in the rosebushes, too much to do, and too little time to do it that's wrenching on your nervous system. Nope. They're not what's doing it. It's your reactions to all those things that creates any stress you feel.

You bring a gang of gremlins into your life and then give them the power to play tug-of-war with your nerves. Like most other problems, stress is shaped only in the mind.

To you, conquering the mountain of insurmountable problems in your life may be like climbing Mt. Everest. To another, coping with the same batch of sticklers would seem like a stroll around the block. It's a matter of personal attitude. In a way, that's promising. Because what is created by thought can be taken apart the same way. You can control stress by learning to manage your attitudes.

Here are some suggestions for doing that.

1. *Use your imagination.*
Tomorrow's dreams make today's problems seem insignificant!

Learn to live a little in your fantasy world. Build a dream, a hope, a pleasant episode for a moment ahead and then feel the joy of fulfillment before the event ever happens! It's OK to daydream. In fact the ability to escape mentally for a while from saw-toothed reality is now accepted as sound therapy, a way to lift disabling stress from the mind.

Fill your thoughts with hope. Look ahead. Always have something pleasurable, something satisfying, or a purpose embracing your entire soul that you can experience at the top of the hill. It will make today's climb seem easy.

2. *Climb a tree.*
Chase squirrels. Move furniture. Dig a hole. Wash the car. Beat a pillow. Sweep a parking lot. Do anything physical when the pressure packs in.

Look at stress as a gift. It's a buildup of energy due to your reaction to a situation. There is only a certain amount of steam you can handle and keep cooking effectively. When that point is exceeded, you need a release valve.

Physical activity helps. Doing nothing hurts, and here's betting you've had a bunch of headaches to prove it.

3. *Hang loose.*

Professional athletes invest hundreds of hours practicing a variety of movements so they can depend on their muscles to react automatically. They know they perform well only when relaxed mentally and physically.

You can put the same principle to work for you. Stay loose. You don't have to rehearse life to live it relaxed. There is no situation or circumstance that will create tension and stress without permission.

Live a day at a time. Don't fight life. It's not a challenge, battle, or struggle. Life is a potential. Everything and everyone is with you, not against you. Accept every circumstance, problem, and event as a gift, an opportunity to experience another dimension of living.

That is the talent of those in their seventies and eighties heading up countries and large organizations. They seem nourished rather than burdened by unresolved conditions. It rests in their attitudes, their composure, and their acceptance of unlived happenings. It is far better to view such concerns as adventures than as calamities.

4. *Know thyself.*

That was good advice in Socrates's time. It's better now with the whirligig tempo of living.

Take time to analyze yourself and your stress patterns. A certain level of stress is beneficial. The human being is like a harp string. Stretch it too tight, and it goes out of tune. But when it's too loose, it makes no music at all. There are both constructive and destructive forms of tension. The management of personal stress begins with knowing which is which.

Only you can do that for you. Monitor your moods. Listen to your body. Hear what it is telling you. Cherish your highs. Walk away from the lows. Most people won't do that. They stubbornly cling to the crazy things that make them feel overloaded.

They're like the fellow who was swindled out of a batch of money by a fraudulent stock scheme. He went to the bunco squad and complained. "Why didn't you come to us before you parted with the funds?" the investigator asked.

"I was afraid you'd advise me not to invest," the victim admitted.

Are you saddled with a load of *should*s and *must*s and *have to*s that are sprinkling grit in your internal cogs? Have you dragged some of those burdens around so long that you feel guilty even considering freeing yourself from them?

5. *Use childlike logic.*
Children are gifted with clear, uncluttered logic. This is often used to puzzle the adult's more distorted thinking.

The little ones delight in displaying their uncomplicated viewpoint of things by asking "Why does the chicken cross the road?" To them it's obvious. To get to the other side, of course.

Or they might tell of the truck that was an inch too high to get under the overpass. What should be done? The grown mind will attempt all sorts of sophisticated approaches while the child is thinking, "Let some air out of the tires."

Then there is the dreadful experience of being locked in the bathroom. Water is pouring into the bathtub with the faucets stuck so they can't be turned off. There are no windows; the heavy door can't be unlocked and fits so tightly that almost no water can escape. Is there a way out, or is drowning inevitable?

Well, you probably remember the response from your childhood days. Why not pull the plug in the bathtub?

Why are such simple approaches to life's puzzles left behind as we grow older?

As you become locked in a space of your own making, with no apparent way to turn off the burdens that are pouring in on you, it seems you'll be drowned in a nervous breakdown. There is no relief to you, the grown-up. For the child the solution is obvious. Why not pull the plug?

Take Inventory

Psychologists dealing with overloaded adults in today's society are prescribing that remedy. People accumulate chores, concerns, obligations, habits, possessions, and overpowering frivolous tasks that tend to suffocate their peace of mind.

Those are termed *stressors.* They are an assortment of subtle complications nailed onto daily schedules that produce destructive stress. The attendant symptoms of sickness, jangled nerves, harsh relationships, and all sorts of other disorders begin erupting.

Current advice is to identify all your stressors and then pull the plug, letting them drain out of your life. That's difficult. The stressors become like barnacles, those hard-shelled crustaceans that foul up a ship's bottom by attaching themselves to its submerged surface.

The stressors affix themselves so adhesively to your existence they seem almost a part of it. To give up these attachments would be like renouncing life itself.

Take an inventory of your stressors by tuning in to your feelings. List all the pet peeves, irritants, aggravating conditions, and people who bug you. Write down everything. Don't omit something because you believe it must be endured as part of a job or relationship.

Don't overlook any area of your existence. Social activities sometimes become social drudgery. Recreation can put pressure on you if you're one who must be the best of the crowd at bridge, tennis, or turning out an afghan. What starts as relaxation can string into tension.

OK. Now you're ready to make choices. Are you going to hang on to the craziness that can make you sick or let it go? You might be surprised at how easy it can be to live your life at your pace and stress tolerances if you're determined.

How It Works

One lady found it so when, near collapse, she added up all the crushing obligations she had allowed to be piled on her shoulders, primarily from the family. Calling a summit conference, she made her declaration of independence, telling them what they could and couldn't expect from her.

It worked out wonderfully! They felt better about doing more for themselves, and she'll live longer.

An executive did the same on a job. The company responded by getting an assistant, reassigning some of the duties, and developing a few larger dimensions to the position. Everyone came out ahead.

If you feel locked in with no way to shut off faucets, floundering in a flood of worries and pressures, try one thing before they rise over your head.

Pull the plug!

Learn to look for the ponies behind your stressors. You cannot go through life changing all the traumatic conditions and circumstances. But you can change your attitude toward them.

Have the courage to set aside the pressures, burdens, and self-imposed obligations and sense the richer joy of feeling in your heart—peace, thankfulness, and happiness.

16

Play Hurt!

It was a closely fought game between two spirited football teams. The Detroit Lions were leading. The Minnesota Vikings were moving toward the goal line to put them ahead. But then Gary Cuozzo, the quarterback, came to the huddle with his left arm dangling loosely at his side.

"You're hurt. We'll take you out," said Bill Brown, the fullback.

"No, leave me in," said Cuozzo. "We've got a drive going."

He stayed in the game with a broken shoulder until the team crossed the goal line. Then he left. This is common among athletes. Pain, soreness, injury, or fatigue exists for which there is no alternative except to "play hurt."

Ken Venturi, the TV golf analyst and former golfer, will always be remembered for playing hurt when he won American golf's highest prize, the U.S. Open title in 1964.

It was hot and muggy on the final day of the tournament at Congressional Golf Course outside Washington, D.C. Venturi was overcome by dehydration. Stretched out on a locker room bench, he was told by a doctor that he would be unable to play that day. But Venturi, sick, weak, and dizzy, played his round barely able to place one foot ahead of the other. It wasn't until the final putt that he sank to his knees, exhausted, muttering, "Thank God, I've won the U.S. Open!" That's playing hurt.

Of similar courage was Bill Emmerton, who in his late forties decided to run 125 miles through Death Valley. He started in the heat of 106 degrees, got thirty miles out, and encountered a sandstorm so severe it blew him off his feet and bounced him fifteen feet along the road. Undaunted, he kept going until he collapsed from sulfur fumes. Following him in a camper, his wife, Norma, thought, "Dear God, this is it."

She soaked his clothes in water, massaged his legs, and three minutes later Emmerton was on his way again. The temperature reached 135 degrees. He finished with the toe of one shoe cut off to allow for the free flow of blood.

"It was like running through hell," he exclaimed. "I suffered, I was in pain. But no one else can stand it as I do!"

In the game of life, decide who or what you are competing against. For day-to-day satisfaction, try just to be better than the person you were yesterday. Accomplish that, and you will always be a winner.

Playing hurt seems to be one of the gutsy qualities of winners. But it is not restricted to athletics. Dwight D. Eisenhower once said, "Ninety percent of everything that will be accomplished today will be done by people who don't feel very good!"

That may not be an accurate statistic, but it is one we can all identify with. There comes a time in our life when there is a task to be done, a job to do, or simply a routine to follow when we do not feel very good. It may be for a day, a week, or a more constant burned-out feeling that leaves us exhausted. This is the time when the challenge presents itself to "play hurt." Life must go on; there is work to be done, opportunities to seize, and the spirit to be restored. Although we all must accept personal responsibility for playing hurt, here are some ideas that might help.

1. *Set your own standards.*
Life is often compared to a game. It does have many of a game's characteristics . . . competition, rules, winning, losing, and choosing to be a spectator or participant.

You can, however, determine your own rules and how you will compete. In fact it is absolutely necessary that you make those decisions if you're going to be a participant rather than merely a spectator in the game of life.

How are you going to compete? There is constructive and destructive competition. When you always have the need to be ahead of someone else, competition has become destructive.

If you're always competing against others, you're training yourself to view people as your adversaries. Life changes from an enjoyable game to a war.

Fortunately, the world seems to be moving away from such intense competition. People are competing against their own personal standards rather than merely trying to beat others. Marathons are a good example. There are hundreds of stories of disabled people running marathons and of people running fifty or a hundred miles only for the inner satisfaction of saying "I did it!"

A New York marathon brought out one such example. On a brisk October morning, more than fifteen thousand turned out for the twenty-six-mile run. Slightly over two hours later the winner completed the race.

Fifty yards from the finish line he looked over his shoulder and saw he had no close competition. He slowed to a trot, waved his arms, and pranced through the tape to the cheers of the crowd and the enjoyment of the TV viewers. Later he told interviewers that he had known at some point that no record would be broken, so there was no reason to put out everything he could.

By 5:30 that evening 13,609 had completed the course, certainly a tribute to their perseverance. The TV evening news reported the results, giving acclaim to all who finished.

Then, at 9:30 that evening, in the quiet of night when there were no TV cameras, no one handing out water or juice, no one cheering or waving banners, the 13,610th person dragged a body that was cut and bruised from falling down across the finish line and fell exhausted. Linda Downs had no more to give. She had completed the twenty-six miles on aluminum crutches. She had been born with cerebral palsy; when the winner skipped across the finish line, she still had more than twenty agonizing miles to go.

Who was the competitor who showed the most courage and character? The one who finished first or the one who finished last?

2. *Play by the rules.*
There are the rules of your game. They might be termed *values.* The quality of your life depends largely on your values.

A true story of a fellow named Tom illustrates the cause and effect of rules and values. Tom was a street kid when he was young. He survived by stealing, taking whatever was available, and getting away with as much as he could. But then they locked him up.

"I was bitter," he said. "I really thought it was OK to steal. That was my way of life. I thought it was unfair that I should get caught when friends I knew were getting away with so much more.

"I got out and started stealing again. But then they locked me up again. That was the story of my life until my thirties. I reached a point where I could not stand being locked up again. I would die if I had to go back to prison.

"I finally woke up. I told myself, 'Tom, you've got the wrong rules. Society is not going to change. As long as you take from somebody else, you're going to suffer. You've got to change.' So I did. I stopped stealing. I don't know why I was so stupid before. But at least my life has a future now that I've changed my rules."

Tom's circumstances were more severe than most people's. But the principle wasn't. The wrong rules get bad results; the right rules get good results. It's that simple.

One more thought. Be careful about the people who are helping you set the rules. There are a lot of losers out there who will try to get you to play the game of life according to their rules. Be your own person. Know yourself—your strengths and your weaknesses. Set your own pace and your own standards. Don't live your life trying to compete with others. You're destined to lose. There will always be someone who owns more than you do and does things better than you do.

3. *Remember that all things pass.*

Long ago an emperor, burdened by worry and despair, called the sages of his kingdom together. "Give me words," he asked, "that I can engrave on my ring that will comfort and guide me through these distressful times."

The wise men spent days searching for the right words that would apply to every situation, setback, and despondent mood. The words they finally gave the emperor were these: "This, too, shall pass away."

More than a hundred years ago an American writer, Paul Hamilton Hayne, heard this fable and wrote a poem entitled "This, too, shall pass away." In it was the line "In all thine anguish lay one truth to heart; this, too, shall pass away."

That line was repeated every morning by Robert Louis Stevenson, whose body was wracked with tuberculosis as he wrote *Treasure Island.* Abraham Lincoln, faced with a nation divided and ravaged by war, reminded himself, "this, too, shall pass away."

When it seems that life is being cruel, unjust, painful, or simply meaningless, look within for the strength to play hurt, remembering that "this, too, shall pass away."

4. *Find your noble purpose.*

Find a noble purpose, a destiny outside your own experience, that inspires you to play hurt and find a loftier meaning to your life.

A good example would be Byron Janis, a world-class

concert pianist. One day he felt a stiffness in his fingers. Medical diagnosis revealed what he feared most—arthritis.

At the peak of his career the disease spread to all his fingers, and the joints of nine of them fused. But he refused to surrender. He kept his ailment a secret from the public. Working long hours practicing new techniques, he continued his concert schedule.

Janis struggled with a variety of medical alternatives, even hypnosis, to handle the pain. His wife gave him therapeutic massages to loosen the stiff joints.

Finally, after twelve years of enduring affliction, he revealed his handicap at a White House concert. He became active in fund-raising for the Arthritis Foundation and continued playing the piano.

Byron Janis was endowed with hope, faith, and a purpose greater than his pain. As he stated: "I have arthritis, but it doesn't have me."

Look within your mind and heart for your spiritual direction. Dream new dreams. Share your life with others, become devoted to serving beyond your own selfish needs. Playing hurt will then be motivational in itself.

5. *Count your blessings.*
Harold Russell was a young paratrooper in World War II. He lost both hands in an accident. Bitter, fearful, and depressed, he lay in his hospital bed drained of any hope for the future. Then he was visited by Charley McGonegal, who had lost his own hands years before. McGonegal shared a quotation by Emerson that had helped him: "For everything you have missed, you have gained something else."

Nourished by that thought, young Russell played hurt while he regained his enthusiasm for life. He went on to become a successful author and actor, winning two Academy Awards. These are but a few of the many who have found new levels of energy, greater dimensions of life, and more magnificent accomplishments by playing hurt. Keep in mind that playing hurt will eventually strengthen, not weaken, your spirit and body.

There are seeds of greatness within you. Discover them, nourish them, let them grow to their fullest potential. Help others do the same for themselves.

The game of life is really one that takes place in your mind; it is determined by your attitudes. You hear a lot about your standards of living; you hear very little about your standards of thinking. They are far more important. For the way you think will be the way you live.

Whatever your pain, adversity, or affliction, look at life and say "There has to be a pony here someplace!" That's learning to play hurt. It's also winning at the game of life!

17

Dare to Grow

In the mountains of Tennessee lived a man who was a laborer six days a week and a preacher on the seventh. The church he served was a small rural congregation tucked far up in the hills. The only compensation he got came from the morning offering. One Sunday he took his six-year-old daughter with him to the service. Just inside the door of the small frame church was a table, and on it rested a collection basket. As they entered, the daughter saw her father place a half-dollar in the wicker basket before any of the congregation arrived.

When the service had ended and the last member had departed, the parson and his daughter started to leave. As they reached the door, both peered expectantly into the collection basket and discovered that the only "take" was the half-dollar he had donated.

After a short silence the little girl said, "You know, Daddy, if you had put more in, you'd have got more out!"

Planter or Picker?

Life is like that. The more you put into it, the more you get out. Why do so many people lack faith in this principle?

They will not invest time and effort in anything that does not pay off quickly. They go through life seeking swift rewards and overnight riches and miss the enormous bounties that are inevitable when they throw themselves into a bigger task with longer-range returns.

The population, it seems, is divided into two groups—the planters and the pickers. There are those who have the patience, confidence, and perseverance to plant an orchard. They fertilize, water, and stand watch as the infant trees shove their antennalike spears through the ground in the struggle to become fruit trees. The guardians protect these young trees from the frost, weeds, insects, and hail until they reach maturity and start bearing fruit.

Now come the fruit pickers. These are the shortsighted ones whose efforts must produce benefits that are quick and obvious, although the returns are far less than for those who planted the orchard.

The planters will have created something of lasting significance that will yield fruit season after season for years to come. The pickers leave nothing behind but bare branches.

The planters, like the child in church, seem intuitively aware that the more they put into life the more they get out. The pickers seem blind to this truth by inclination or choice and go wandering through life forever seeking the fast fortune.

People Are Like Apples

A green apple is very contented just being a green apple. But alas! As long as it stays attached to a tree branch, it must keep working to grow into a ripe red apple. The only way it can possibly remain a green apple is to fall off the tree. Even then it would be short-lived as a green apple because it would gradually waste away.

The same is true of the milkweed seed. The delight of its existence is bursting from its pod and being carried aloft by the silky floss that serves as its very own airline.

Airborne it floats about, freeloading on the lacy puff that lets the breeze decide the adventure of the day.

But then the air quiets. The seed settles to the ground. There it becomes captured by the earth, where it must start toiling to grow into pale green leaves and purplish flowers. The seed can no longer drift about just contented as a seed. When held in place by the earth, it is committed. It must grow. It has no choice.

The human being is not much different from the green apple or milkweed seed. Where there is no attachment, no commitment, there is no growth. But once an individual is held in place, dedicated by choice or necessity to face every problem, all challenges, the highs and lows of each day, growth is inevitable.

Be Committed

I was the dinner speaker at a banquet in Chicago honoring employees who had been with the large national corporation for twenty-five years or more. I sat beside the newly elected president at the head table. He had started as a clerk with the company eighteen years before.

I looked out over the ballroom at the four hundred people busily chatting and eating their dinners. I turned to him and asked, "I'm curious. You started with the company eighteen years ago. Every person in the room has been with the organization longer than you have, many surely starting in positions ahead of you. Yet you went by all of them and became president. How come?"

"I'd like to make it sound complicated," he said. "But it isn't. It's commitment. I'll bet there's not a single person here tonight who expected to be here when they first started. To them it was a job that just kept going on from year to year.

"Not me. The day I came to this company I made the decision I would never leave. No matter how I was treated, what they asked me to do, how much I was paid, I'd spend the rest of my working life right here. So whatever my assignment, I did it the very best I could. I had to. I had nowhere else to go. While everybody else was putting in their time from week to week wondering what they would do with their lives, I knew. I was committed. So I passed up a lot of people along the way."

He was a planter. He was also a green apple fastened to a limb, a milkweed seed held close to the earth. There was no alternative except to become what he was capable of becoming. That's growth.

His was an unusual attitude, admittedly not suitable for everyone. Some people laze along in life, going from place to place, and when they encounter difficulty they leave the situation and move into something else. Some are convinced that's the way to live. However, there is little or no personal growth or progress.

There are those who argue that change is good. Why put up with trying situations? OK. We all have to figure out what's best for ourselves. But if you feel a gnawing compulsion that demands outstanding achievement, an inner quest to cope with any situation, a drive to accomplish any goal that your mind can conceive and believe, you must remain fastened to any given set of circumstances long enough to rise above all the problems that come churning forth.

That's commitment. It's also a way to grow.

Plant the Seeds of Your Strengths

Tom Sawyer and Huckleberry Finn might never have been known the world over if their originator, Mark Twain, had not remained committed to his talents and ignored his weaknesses. Twain never clearly understood the complexities of punctuation. One of his manuscripts was sent back to him by the publisher with the request that it be punctuated correctly.

The author returned it untouched. He also enclosed a generous assortment of colons, semicolons, commas, hyphens, exclamation points, question marks, and periods with these instructions:

"I am enclosing all the punctuation marks required for my manuscript. Please insert as you see fit."

Twain sensed within him the ability to write. He never allowed his ignorance of punctuation to hold him back from developing that ability.

The Challenge of Growth

Ever notice a strange feature of the achievements of many great people? They had to come from farther back than most to win the race of expressing their talents. But they persisted, never deviating from becoming what they were destined to become.

That's growth, personal growth toughened by adversity and self-reliance. You can see it in a flower, alone, searching for moisture and dirt in the crevice of a rock. Still, every day those petals open for the sun's nourishing beams. Born within is a need to grow, to fulfill its destiny.

Or a young bird falls from the nest. Those fragile, untaught wings flap instinctively as it scoots for the protection of a bush. Food or warmth is unimportant; this life must fly to survive!

There may be an important lesson there. To untangle the mysteries of the possibilities within us we must face a stone wall, a barrier. No more casting about, running, or turning back. Now is the time to rely only on yourself. This is when personal growth begins.

The Way to Become Strong

Growth, breaking from the barriers of the past, is not easy. In fact it can be a burdensome, trying struggle. It often takes restraint to stand by and let it happen.

A friend, Gene MacKay, moved his family onto a farm rather than live in one of the more congested areas of New York State. He told of one of his children watching ducklings emerge from their shells. One was having difficulty. So the child, in her anxiety and love, helped the tiny bundle of fuzzy feathers from its shell. Two hours later the duckling was dead. The others survived strong and healthy.

"We know," said Gene, "if we help a bird from its shell during the birth process it will die or always be weak and unhealthy."

Birds, like people, have a destiny, an inborn capacity. Theirs is to fly. Growing to achieve this is difficult. Yet, however strenuous it may be for an egg to turn into a bird, it would be a great deal harder for it to learn to fly while remaining an egg!

How high can you learn to fly? It depends on your self-development, your initiative, dedication, and desire.

What Are You Becoming?

Growth is an inseparable element of the universe. All substance is on a course of becoming something.

An acorn is becoming an oak tree.

Coal will, in some aeon, harden into a diamond.

So why should growth be so difficult for a human being to understand?

The human being is the only particle of creation that is given a body and a mind that does not know specifically what it is capable of becoming. A petunia seed knows it is supposed to become a petunia. But a human being is only barely perceptive of the wonders resting within the mind.

The unending discoveries of the magnificent powers of the mind are, to me, growth. Uncovering the mind's unlimited capacities for learning, feeling, knowing, sensing, and doing things it has never done before can be rich growth experiences.

Learning you can love another person more with every passing day and year is growth.

Finding out you can sell when you thought that all you could ever be was a grave digger could be growth.

Catching sight of some new goals and striving toward them can be growth.

Detecting that you can be better at what you're doing can be growth.

Trying and discovering—that's growth.

That word *trying* is the barrier to growth. Because trying means failing. But failing becomes increasingly distasteful with the accumulation of years. That's why the bulk of human growth occurs early in life. And, according to many experts, that shriveling tendency opens the door to boredom, discontent, sickness, and even death.

Stop growing and you start dying. Instead, cast about you for opportunities to grow. Look within and bring to sight the unnoticed compartments of your self. Try doing things you have never done before.

All Development Is Self-Development

Personal growth is often confused with learning. Learning comes from the exploration of skills and information outside of yourself. But when experience, talent, knowledge, feelings, and intuitions are appraised through the heart and mind, that's personal growth. It can be achieved only by turning within.

This process is triggered best by asking questions of yourself. Some people never grow much because they always go outside of themselves for the answers to their problems. They ask their employer, "What will be my future?"

"Why don't you make me feel more needed, wanted, and loved?" they may inquire of family and friends.

The night schools, seminars, and bookstore shelves containing self-help books attract people in droves, all of them wondering how they can be more successful. Few realize they have all they need within them. Questions can activate that potential.

You might start with these.

Do you have as much money or success as you would like to have? After responding to that question, go on to the next one.

Are you doing as good a job as you know how to? Come on now; be honest.

OK, here's the next one: why not? Let those two words

roll around for a while. Some lights might go on in a few dark corners of your mind. You could be led into asking "How can I do better?" Think about holding on to that as a permanent prod for getting ahead in life.

Do you see what's happening? Those queries will arouse an awareness of your inner qualities. Do you want to keep doing exactly what you're doing now for the rest of your life?

What are your hopes, dreams, goals? Most people never realize the possibilities of their lives because they don't answer questions like those. Surprising things happen when they do.

Many want something of their own, a business or an independent career. The faltering allow themselves to be held back, believing they need more education, ability, or financial backing.

Set Aside Fears

One of the most common barriers to putting every bit of effort and energy into a task is the haunting question "What will people think?"

Therein lies one of the greatest limitations of human talent and achievement. "I am afraid of what people might think!"

That delusion stalking about in the mind restricts people from speaking in front of others, from becoming salespeople, from writing, painting, singing, venturing forth with their ideas—in short, from discovering all that they can do and become.

"What will people think?" Where did such a ghost, one that haunts and holds people back for a lifetime, originate? Perhaps it was part of childhood.

Bonaro Overstreet, the psychologist, wrote, "Parents tell children so often that it will be a great disappointment if they do not measure up. They virtually force children into an exaggerated fear of failure, and into an exaggerated self-dislike where failure occurs."

Charles Kettering, former director and research consultant for General Motors, seems to agree. In an address he once said, "A study indicated that the more education a person has, the less likely that person will be an inventor. Now the reason is quite simple. From the time boys and girls start in school, they are examined several times a year. It is a very, very disastrous thing to fail. An inventor fails all the time and triumphs only once.

"I can take a group of young people anyplace and teach them to be inventors if I can get them to throw off the hazard of being afraid to fail."

To experience the fullest measure of life you must first expose yourself as a novice. To skate you begin by wobbling, staggering, and falling down. Awkwardness and ineptitude always precede the development of a talent.

What are the risks? How "foolish" can one appear to be? What do people really think?

You don't have to be the best or even good at anything to participate in life. Just have the courage to try. Measure yourself not against others but by your own progress.

Don't hold yourself back from discovering what you can be out of fear of "what people will think." John J. Audubon might have said it best: "The woods would be very silent if no birds sang there except those that sang best."

18

Getting Cooperation from Others

Narcissus, in ancient Greek mythology, was the son of the river god Cephisus. Proud and handsome, he was the object of many girls' love. The nymph Echo was one of them. But Narcissus was indifferent toward such affection. Echo was so hurt by his coldness that all but her voice faded away.

The gods, angered by this, condemned Narcissus to fall in love with his own reflection in a pool of water. He became so in love with himself that he could not leave the pool. There he died as he gazed incessantly at his reflection and was changed into the flower named *narcissus*.

Derived from the fable is the term *narcissism*, used to describe those excessively fascinated by themselves.

People Are Looking into Pools

That, to some degree, identifies the adult population. Especially today. For it has become fashionable to read the latest book or go to a seminar to find out "who you are."

Watching out for number one, getting in touch with yourself, and becoming aware of the real you are the modern symbols of sophistication and "putting your life together."

Printing presses are harvesting reams of books and tests that can take people apart and put them back together in tidy little squares or more elaborate profiles. Their popularity seems endless as people are lured into looking into the pool of clear water and gazing at their psychological images.

The pursuit of all the possible reflections is also endless. For the individual is, in fact, many individuals. Each is like a little ball of clay with hundreds of impressions made by friends, family, parents, and experiences. New balls of clay are constantly being formed and old ones remolded. They are all linked together in a complex fashion from which emerges a slightly different person in each of life's experiences.

Little wonder that, like Narcissus, people stare into the mirror of the world and become obsessed with the reproductions of themselves. It is a constant source of mystical intrigue.

Life in the Future

Consider, for a moment, the very successful few who seem to have separated themselves from their narcissistic urges. They are less curious about who they are than who they can be.

They do not spend their lives in a confused quest to understand the configuration and nature of the inner balls of clay. Regardless of what they have been, their inner selves can be assembled, put together, and molded into the creation of the beholder.

The enlightened don't waste time gawking at images in the pool. That only reflects what has been. What will be can be the exciting reality of tomorrow.

You have within you the power to determine what you will be. But first, have the strength to leave the pool and avoid changing permanently into the flower that you are now, like Narcissus.

Focus on What You Can Be

That means deciding what you want from life. Look around you. Pick your models of people who are what you want to be. Stamp those impressions indelibly in your mind. Visualize them. Give your energy to them.

Depart from all the excessive concerns about your own happiness, health, comfort, and treatment by others. Does that mean not being proud of who you are? No. It means falling in love with life and people rather than yourself.

You will discover a wondrous plan for your life; miracles will follow miracles if you can break away from the morbid fascination of who you are. Then get busy with the visions of what you can be.

Get Outside of Yourself

Only by forgetting yourself are you remembered. By giving yourself away you find yourself. Only through acts of love to others do you surrender the burdens you have piled on yourself.

That is taught in an old Chinese tale about a woman whose only son died. In distress she went to a holy man and pleaded, "What mystic powers do you have that will lift the ache from my heart?"

Rather than reason with her, he said, "Fetch me a mustard seed from a home that has never known sorrow. We will use it to drive the pain from your life." The woman set out in search for the miracle seed.

She approached a stately mansion, knocked on the door, and said, "I am seeking a home that has never known sadness. Is this such a place?"

"You have come to the wrong home," she was told.

Then followed a description of tragedy and hopelessness that had befallen the residents.

The woman thought to herself, "Who is more able to help these desperate people than I, who has also known such pain?" So she stayed and comforted them.

She went on, seeking a home that had never known sorrow. But wherever she went, from the simplest to the grandest of lodgings, she found stories of suffering and misfortune. In each instance she stayed long enough to share and minister to the other people's grief.

In so doing she forgot about her quest for the magical mustard seed, never realizing it had, in fact, driven the sorrow out of her life.

It is a reminder that we find the meaning of life when concentrating on others' wants rather than thinking only of ourselves.

Find Others' Needs

There is an ancient Persian saying that expresses the idea more specifically: "If you seek a brother to share your burden, brothers are in truth hard to find. But if you are in search of someone whose own burden you will yourself share, there is no scarcity of such brothers."

There, in words of ancient wisdom, is the invisible key to peak performance in working with others. Look to others to solve your problems of earning money, selling goods and services, finding security or happiness, and you will find few to join you. Go to others with an honest heart to help them find joy, love, happiness, success, and prosperity, and an endless multitude begins to appear.

Those who give attract; those who take repel.

Positive attracts; negative repels. That is an infallible law in the world of thought.

Success is yours in relationships and a career if you understand that simple principle and exert your energies and mentality, without exception, toward its application.

What do the words mean?

Start first with what you want from life. Would you have riches? Family and friends? Distinguished achievement? Whatever you name, there is one inescapable requirement for the realization of your dreams.

You need people to help you.

You will attract others with whom you can share your faith, your knowledge, your skills. And when you do that, another unit of power will be added to your combined energies. Goals will be set. Success is now attainable! And so hope will emerge.

Hope attracts; doubt repels.

You will then be the mentor of others. Together you will share your fortunes and setbacks, the ups and downs, the bright moments and the discouragements. You will work closely—not for selfish gain or martyred commitment but because you care for one another. This, then, becomes the greatest law of all.

Love attracts; selfishness repels.

19

How to Be a Winner

The trained instincts of your mind can hold you back from experiencing the unlimited nature of life. Why is it that with such an available abundance of wealth, success, love, adventure, health, and all the other potentials of living the human being seems driven to get as little as possible rather than as much as possible?

To answer that, think of your own life for a moment. Didn't you start playing games that emphasized winning or losing at an early age? You probably learned something about competing with others that didn't stop with the fun and frolic of kid games. It extended into a classroom. Who got the best grades? Who could draw the best, write the neatest, spell the most accurately, sing the prettiest, and learn the fastest? Who was the most attractive, popular, witty, and likely to succeed? This comparison process was really a form of competition. After all, only one person could win. The same rivalry existed in being accepted or having friends. There was often competition for the friendship of another or for acceptance into some sort of peer group.

And was there ever a child in a family who did not feel, at some time, a little less loved by a parent than a brother or sister?

139

Competition Lives On

When school days were over, the sense of rivalry simply deepened. Driving an automobile can be a contest in which other drivers are your adversaries—honking their horns at you, slowing you down, getting in your way, or occupying all the convenient parking spaces.

Consider, in addition, the stronger impact on your attitudes of competition for career positions, wages, and places to live. In almost every instance the viewpoints that there are only a few high-paying jobs and that it's difficult to find a place to live where you will be happy are hammered into your thinking.

A shadow falls over your attitudes, through which you view others as your rivals or contestants with whom you must compete for the limited supply of earth's riches or the love, adventure, and successes of life. There are few winners. Most have to settle for what they can get.

But it needn't be that way. You can be a winner. Everyone can. First, remind yourself that what you hold in your mind you will eventually experience in your life. If your thinking is contaminated with rivalry, competition, envy, losing out, or settling for less than the boundless qualities of life, then that is what you will inevitably experience. If, on the other hand, your consciousness is filled with thoughts of prosperity, love, success, and endless joy, then those will be the characteristics of your life. Know that the entire Earth is yours to enjoy.

The love that fills your life with warmth and excitement is not what others give you but what you feel for others. There need be no restrictions or restraints on that.

Remove all thoughts of competing with those around you. The only sure way of being a winner is to help others become winners. Life is not a battle or contest. It is a potential. The ultimate victory of life is to win the absolute maximum of your personal potential. You will never know what that is without the help of the people around you. To be a winner, help them be winners.

You can win by helping others win.

Help Others Be Right

You can get out of the competing trap by helping people be right rather than trying to make them wrong.

"You're right!" Those are probably the most powerful words in the English language when dealing with others.

The human being, you see, lacks the protective equipment of other forms of life. People are not large like elephants, do not run as cheetahs, are missing the shells of turtles, fangs of wolves, needles of porcupines, stench of skunks, or venom of snakes.

In prehistoric ages a superior mind was the device the human relied on for survival. The mind, however, lacked many of the instincts of other organisms to distinguish danger. It had to evaluate life-threatening situations and conceive solutions.

In other words, the head had to be right! This characteristic was not left behind in the cave. The human mind still believes it must be right to survive.

You have no trouble with that when brushing your teeth, buying shoes, weeding a flower bed, or choosing a flavor of ice cream. But how about relating to others? Like children, your spouse, people at work, or neighbors whose kids are running through your pansy patch? For you to be right, at least a few times (or quite a few!) they have to be wrong.

You tend to make others losers instead of winners. Observe, for instance, the sickness that plagues our freeways. Shootings, horn honking, obscene gestures, and physical violence occur as ways of telling another driver, "You're driving wrong."

I'm Right! You're Wrong!

There has never been a soul who has not at some time felt underappreciated and overworked. To allow that feeling to grow is to go to some strong extremes to prove that others are wrong. That, then, justifies feelings of self-pity. Alas! How many careers are detoured and marriage relationships aborted by the tenacious struggle to be right when one's self-righteousness is threatened?

The futility of hanging on to the "I'm right! You're wrong!" syndrome almost always prevails. It is rarely achieved in relationships. Think, for a moment, about the last disagreement you had with someone. Who was right? You were, weren't you? And the more you thought about it, the more right you became. And, odds are, the other person was hanging on to the same conviction of being right.

Here's a simple suggestion for turning this bias around and making it work for you rather than against you. Help the other person be right! When confronted by a situation in which you are tempted to attack another's view, say to yourself, "I'm wrong. You're right." You don't have to hang on to it forever. Just hold it in your mind long enough to see the other person's perspective.

If there is a difference of opinion with another, don't fall into the "I'm right. You're wrong" trap. Instead, work toward determining *what* is right, rather than *who* is right. In fact, those are velvetlike words to open negotiations. Try suggesting "It's not important to prove who is right or who is wrong. What we want to decide is what is right and go from there."

People are rarely totally wrong or totally right. Find the ways that others are right and stress those points. You will find others much less adamant about defending their differences with you.

Avoid sentences that imply that you are going to get into an "I'm right. You're wrong" stance. Here are a few of those:

"You should have. . . ."
"I knew this would happen."
"Why didn't you . . . ?"
"You neglected to. . . ."
"If you had mentioned that before. . . ."
"This never would have happened if you had. . . ."
"You were supposed to. . . ."

Remember that in almost all instances of differences of

opinion you are not dealing with facts. You are dealing with attitudes and views.

Avoid the "Gotcha Game"

The "Gotcha Game" is an interesting activity motivated by the smug desire to be right and make another wrong. It is best illustrated by two golfers standing on the first tee, discussing a wager on the game. One, a considerably better player than the other, asked, "How many strokes do I have to give you?"

"None," the other replied. "All I want are a couple of 'gotchas'!"

"What are those?"

"I'll explain as we go around."

Delighted that he didn't have to give any strokes, the hustler prepared to invade the wallet of the pigeon. He addressed the ball, waggled his club, and started the club back. Just at the top of the backswing came a blustery "Gotcha!" from the opponent.

The ball, badly hit, sliced into the rough.

The duffer smugly announced, "That was the first 'gotcha.' Remember, I've got another one coming."

Shaken and distracted for the rest of the round waiting for another *gotcha*, the better golfer was beaten soundly.

Highways are exhilarating playgrounds for Gotcha Games. When you're driving a car too slowly or flipping the wrong directional signal, a *gotcha* could be forthcoming. It might be a few horn blasts, an obscene gesture, or, where the game is more seriously played, a rifle shot. As in other games, tempers can become inflamed, and the *gotcha*s take the shape of physical violence.

Gotcha players in restaurants are like kittens with balls of yarn. Being too slow, not pleasant enough, or spilling a few drops of coffee can trigger an "Aha! Gotcha!" that may not be verbalized but is reflected in the size of the tip. Or food can always be sent back to the kitchen. My wife and I were dining one evening and saw one dedicated Gotcha player send the same food back three times and then change the order completely.

The Gotcha Game has become so popular that companies are spending millions of dollars building their own playgrounds, usually called customer service departments. Most of the customers they service have justifiable *gotchas*. On the other hand, there are fervent Gotcha players who unreasonably vent their hostilities on a company with myriad tormenting *gotchas*.

Be a Winner

Here is an observation that might be helpful if you're considering the Gotcha Game. There are no winners. That's right. There are only losers.

Your life is not made better by attacking others. Nor do you suddenly become right by making others wrong.

The chief cause of sour human relationships is that people are not acting the way others think they should act. They are also human. They make mistakes. They usually feel awful about them. And those are the playthings of the Gotcha Game.

Only they are not really playthings. They are people's emotions. And if those feelings are wounded with *gotchas*, no one comes out ahead. It's something to think about the next time you're tempted to play the Gotcha Game.

It is far better to help people be right than to look for ways to make them wrong. It is a profound objective of a human relationship. But it works! It makes your life better!

You become a winner helping others become winners. That's a wonderful way to relate!

20

Everything Can Be Beautiful

A fable in Eastern folklore tells about a farmer who was wandering along a country road looking anxiously at the road before him. A neighbor saw him and asked, "Is something troubling you, my friend?"

"My horse ran away," the farmer replied.

"Oh, that's too bad!" the neighbor exclaimed.

"Is it?" the farmer responded.

The next day the two met again. "Did you find your horse?" the neighbor inquired.

"Yes," the farmer replied.

"Oh, that's good!" the neighbor said.

"Is it?" the farmer uttered.

The next day they met again. "How is your horse?" asked the neighbor.

"A bit wild," the farmer mentioned. "He threw my son, and my son broke his leg."

"Oh, that's too bad," the neighbor said.

"Is it?" the farmer asked.

The next time they met, the country had gone to war. The farmer explained that all young men were drafted into the army. His son was exempt because of his broken leg.

It is a quaint little anecdote with the rather profound

philosophy that events in life are good or bad only according to one's perspective.

How Do You Deal with Your "Horses That Run Away"?

Every incident, every experience, every trifling episode links together to evolve into greater meaning. Each is a cause for a trailing effect. Knowing that, you can choose what those effects will be. Approaching each day with a positive attitude can make growth and worthy purpose the effects of daily living.

Who is to say that the lost sale, sniffly nose, flat tire, and irritating rebuke are incidents that must be labeled as "too bad"?

Perhaps the lost sale will be a learning experience from which ten more sales will come. Or it might lead to an extra measure of determination with far greater rewards than just the single sale.

Maybe the sniffly nose prompts a few hours of rest when a good book is read or a bright idea is generated. Or it might be only a gentle reminder that glowing health is indeed a blessing that needs mental and physical nourishment.

The flat tire disabled the auto only for a time. How fortunate that it was not a blowout that could cause a serious accident. Or was it the opportunity to realize the goodness of others when a stranger stopped and offered to help?

That irritating rebuke may have a splinter of justification. There are ways to respond other than to attack or defend.

Those two are the customary responses, aren't they? Either the other person must be attacked, or the rebuke must be proved untrue. Neither works.

How about listening, thanking the other, and then pondering the critical remark for a time? If it has no validity, then merely forgive and forget. On the other hand, there may be an objective in sight that can lead to substantial personal growth.

Choose Positive Attitudes

Most important, don't allow what appear to be minor setbacks destroy your day. Above all, don't look back with remorse and self-pity. A prominent psychologist recently said that the majority of his patients would not be in his office if they could avoid the words "What if . . . ?"

If they were to stop looking back and creating worry, sorrow, and "poor me" pictures with their illusions of "what if," they would not be mired in their psychological swamps of despair.

So much for those events that one might evaluate like the farmer's neighbor by saying "Oh, that's too bad."

How about the incident that might be viewed by exclaiming "Oh, that's good!"

The farmer's comment "Is it?" might be worth considering. Much can be learned by dealing with the good happenings in life. Are they shared? Are they stepping-stones to more significant events? Are they accepted with humility and thankfulness?

Anyone can handle failure. Millions do it day after day. But it requires remarkable wisdom, maturity, and unselfishness to wear the cloak of success. Particularly challenging when a certain measure of success is achieved is not to view success as a parking lot for lethargy and complacency.

So hold fast to your positive attitudes toward life's constant stream of events. William Shakespeare expressed it another way when he wrote:

"There is nothing either good or bad, but thinking makes it so."

It is your perception of a situation that determines whether it is good or bad, positive or negative. Your perception of life, in fact, determines your experiences, emotions, and thoughts. Each person's perception is different and unique. For example:

Why Kill Dandelions?

The dandelion is really quite a lovely plant. The golden yellow head is a cluster of petals surrounded by leaves that can be used in salads or cooked as greens. It is a remarkable source of nutritious vitamins and minerals.

The early colonists brought what was known to the French as the *dent de lion* to America from Europe. But then there were those who were able to convince others that this was not actually a graceful, useful bit of herbage but rather an ugly weed.

"How ridiculous," I thought at one time. So I let dandelions grow freely in my yard. And I enjoyed their robust appearance and hearty zest for living.

Then I sold that home. The new owners immediately killed all my dandelions.

Obviously their perception of the situation was different from mine. Theirs, fortunately, dictated that they kill only plants. There are those whose perceptions justify killing other people. Or condemning, judging, hating, failing, and, yes, succeeding, hoping, and loving.

How we behave or feel is designed largely by our perceptions. What makes us all unique is the magic that our minds perform with those perceptions. For the mind perceives things not as they are but as they should be.

So we perceive our children not as they are but as they should be. And that's the way it is with spouses, friends, customers, jobs, and the daily trickle of all conditions and experiences.

How the Eyes Perceive

The lens in the eye inverts images so they are cast on the back of the eye upside down. The mind, though, has learned to interpret the images as they should be.

A university developed special glasses that made the world appear upside down. When subjects wore them for a couple of days, their minds learned to make corrections, and images appeared as they should.

When they took the glasses off, however, everything again appeared upside down until the mind relearned to interpret the pictures as they should be.

Dandelions are of little consequence. But careers, relationships, attitudes, and physical conditions are not. And perceptions are just as influential in those areas.

There is no job or activity that has any meaning at all. Your perception determines the meaning. Your mind decides if your career is satisfying or frustrating, fulfilling or boring, interesting or dull.

Your mind will perceive things not as they are but as they should be.

The greatest frustration in personal relationships is that people perceive others not as they are but as they should be.

Companies are discovering that they're coming up short on sales because of viewing customers not as they are but as they should be. That goes for employees too, which causes some snarled relationships.

But, then, employees look at the company not as it is but as it should be. And that causes them to feel jerked around a bit. Maybe the companies and employees could get closer on their perceptions.

You Can Change Your Life

Knowing the mechanics of perceptions can transform a life. In fact that is the only way to transform a life.

You can choose the manner in which you perceive your world. Is it positive or negative? Are there hopes and possibilities in every situation? Is there goodness and love in every person? Is your body designed perfectly to serve you in health and vigor?

If those are your attitudes, the mind will execute for you in magnificent fashion.

For it will perceive things not necessarily as they are, for things have no meaning in themselves, but as they should be according to your attitudes.

How do you perceive horses that run away? Is the dandelion a weed or a flower? By choosing your perceptions you are creating your reality. Whatever you perceive you will experience.

Look for others to take advantage of you, and your suspicion will seem to set the whole world against you.

Look for others to act negatively in your presence, and their every act will appear tainted with sourness.

Look for the shortcomings of your children, and with diabolical certainty they will seem to magnify.

Look for your business dealings to be sparse and fruitless, and all those you meet will seem to be guiding you into the breadlines.

Dwell on the countless times your mate has ignored your tender feelings and—horrors!—you find yourself with a total stranger.

Thankfully, the principle is equally valid for its positive applications.

Let your mind linger on the kind, joyful moments of a marriage, and it's amazing how the other person seems to change.

Look for the common interest and concerns of others, and strangers quickly become friends.

Expect that every contact made with another is going to be mutually productive and helpful and for some mysterious reason you suddenly will become adept at business dealings.

It's not easy to build relationships by managing your thoughts rather than merely reacting to others. But it can be done. The rewards are rich and meaningful.

21

Practice Love

Remember the story of the stable boy who saw nothing but manure and cried out, "Wow! There has to be a pony here someplace!"

So it is with life. Behind the illusions of suffering, obstacles, despair, and difficulties, there are ponies. There are opportunities for self-discovery and fresh visions, discarding the old and being reborn into the new.

Pause, look around you, and be thankful for the scores of gifts received daily. Don't be like the man who died, went to heaven, and was asked by God, "How did you like my world?"

"I don't really know," replied the man. "I was on the telephone."

The phone, TV, and other distractions can shield us from the larger gifts of life. Imagine, for example, the extravaganza there would be if only one sunset occurred every ten years; multitudes would swarm out to see it. Yet that is exactly what happens. No two sunsets or sunrises are exactly alike. The same is true of each tree, bush, or flower. All have their individual shapes, characters, and stories to tell. Their differences are what make them interesting and beautiful.

People Are Unique

People are like that. Each one is different. That's what makes them interesting and beautiful. Why does the human mind seem annoyed by and critical of the differences in people? Uniqueness is one of life's most profound gifts for each person—as long as it is viewed as a gift.

The way to view uniqueness in a positive way is through love. Love your neighbor as yourself. Love your enemies. Love! Love! Love! The "pony" in any of life's situations is the gift of love—giving it and receiving it.

For love must be given to be received. There is a philosophy of life that dictates that whatever you give out you get back. What goes around comes around. That law of cause and effect provides the joy and fulfillment of life as well as the misery and pain.

If you express anger and hostility, that's what you will get. If not from others, then you will experience it in your body and affairs. Criticize and condemn others, and you will most certainly inherit the same unpleasantries in some fashion yourself. What you do to others you are essentially doing to yourself. It is a law of life.

Love Yourself

You are reminded to love. For if that is what you give, then that is what you will receive. Love can be expressed in endless ways. Understanding, serving, sharing, listening, praising, helping, smiling, and being the best you know how to be are all ways to love.

Love yourself. Modern science reveals that a majority of the pains of life are self-inflicted. Sickness, poverty, bruised relationships, and hopelessness can be caused by not liking yourself. Careers and marriages can be distorted tragically by lack of self-esteem.

Don't be afraid to look into the mirror and say you love that person looking back at you. Whatever the past has been, it is past. Make the most of now by loving your uniqueness, your talents, your good qualities. Unburden yourself from all your mistakes and weaknesses of the past by loving who you are now.

Love Works

If there is one absolute law of life etched in the annals of existence of this planet whirling through space, it is this: love works; hate doesn't.

Love makes your life better, more joyful. All that is good and lovely about life comes from love. Life can never be experienced in its infinite potential without love.

Hate, on the other hand, creates pain, sickness, misery, and all the other despairs of life. That is an irrefutable fact proven scientifically and in the chronicles of humanity. Hate causes all the wars and tragedies that mortals impose on themselves.

Hate, held in your heart, inevitably produces suffering. It poses in many forms . . . prejudice, criticism, judgment, resentment, envy, and all the other assorted dislikes toward others.

Loving, completely and wholly, strengthens and pro longs life. Very simply, from love comes health and from hate comes sickness. In fact hate *is* sickness.

Little Hates Hurt

Just about all who read this imagine they are "loving" people. And they are. They have friends, are nice to people, get along with others at work, care about their families, and are sympathetic to the sorrows of others. So they say "See? I love others. So how come I've got this ulcer and have headaches all the time?"

Well, our problem is that the love we feel within does not immunize us from the damaging effects of all of our little hates. And the hates that pile up and injure our bodies are not the big ones for the scoundrels we read about in the papers but rather the little ones for the people we love the most.

It is the aggravation and frustration we feel because our children are doing things they shouldn't, the resentment and anger that build because our spouses are not acting or treating us the way we think they should, the hostility for the bosses who are insensitive and unappreciative, or the mild rage that smolders when we feel cheated or not served adequately by others. In short, the hates that hurt are all the envies, blames, grudges, criticisms, judgments, conflicts, angers, and resentments that we stock up in our minds and emotions day after day.

What We Do to Ourselves

We're crazy, aren't we? It's absolutely insane what we do to ourselves by allowing these thoughts to pile up within us and come out in our bodies as lumps and aches and pains and sicknesses! When will we ever learn that what we think others are doing to us we're really doing to ourselves?

We get angry and say "You make me sick!" Wrong. *We* make us sick. Not sometimes. Always!

How do we get rid of our hates? The only lasting antidote to hate is love. That means learning to love when we feel least like loving. When you sense irritation, criticism, blame, or resentment creeping into your feelings, quick, start loving.

The Hard Way Is Easy

It isn't easy. But there's an expression that the hard way becomes easy and the easy way becomes hard. It's like the story of a huge bully sauntering into a dimly lit saloon. "Is there anybody here named Kilroy?" he snarled. There was a moment of silence, and then a little Irishman stepped forward. "I'm Kilroy," he said.

The tough guy picked him up and threw him across the bar. Then he punched him in the jaw, kicked him,

slapped him around, and walked out. About fifteen minutes later the little fellow came to. "Boy, did I fool him," he
said. "I ain't Kilroy."

It's easy for us to pretend to be Kilroy, to make believe
we're always loving, covering up all our little hates. But
after a while we suffer as they eat away at our minds and
bodies. The easy way becomes hard.

An alternative would be facing every encounter with
those about us with love, saying to ourselves, "No one or
no situation has the power to stop me from loving. I will
not allow thoughts of criticism, doubt, anger, blame, or
resentment to occupy my mind. I love this person I'm
dealing with right now. Nothing can keep me from doing
that." That's hard at first. But after a while the hard way
becomes easy as loving becomes the habitual response to
all of life's situations, healing and blossoming into joy,
peacefulness, and perfect health.

Learn to Love

To live is to love; a life without love is really no life at all.
Love is an energy; it dissolves problems, heals, nurtures,
restores, and bonds one life to another.

The human being is born with the ability to love.
There seems to be an inborn tendency to love one another,
family members, and the world within which we live.

But there can be more than that! Love can also be
developed. The more loving you become, the richer your
life becomes. The quality and depth of life are in direct
proportion to the degree to which you learn to love.

Each individual must determine the specific way to
love. Here are some ideas for becoming a more loving
person:

1. *Love unconditionally.*
Learn to look beyond the actions and behavior of others
and care for them. Loving should not depend on the way
another treats you. Just love.

In Japan, tucked high in the mountains, is an area

known as "The Place Where You Leave Your Mother." Centuries ago it was believed that the old and feeble were taken there and left to die.

The story is told about the strong young son carrying a small frail mother up the mountains to leave her there. He noticed that she wanted to stop frequently. Each time, she would gather some sticks and break them.

Finally he asked, "Why, Mother, do you leave a trail of broken sticks?"

"So you won't lose your way coming back, my son," replied the mother.

It is a fable of love, a mother's love. That is loving unconditionally. It is a gift of the spirit, a potential of every individual.

In the days ahead, practice loving to help others find their way. Your acts of love, like broken sticks, can provide guidance for others. Give your love without thought of what you will be getting in return. Love unconditionally.

2. *Try the thirty-day love test.*
Ernestine Schumann-Heink, the immortal operatic contralto, appeared on the world's concert stages and opera houses from 1879 to 1926. Before each appearance she would stand off stage, close her eyes, visualize the audience, and repeatedly state, "I love you." That simple statement empowered her performance and its effect on the audience.

You can develop the same charismatic energy by repeating those words. For the next thirty days, practice thinking "I love you" with every encounter with another.

Meet the scowls of strangers with that thought. Before every customer contact, utter those words to yourself. No matter what disagreement or difference you have with another, counter with "I love you."

Avoid criticizing, judging, or condemning any other person. Just replace those thoughts with "I love you."

Do this for thirty days. If you find that you have forgotten to repeat the statement, then start the thirty days over

again. Practice it until you've replaced every negative attitude toward another with "I love you." Do it for thirty days
and you're on your way to an extra dimension of love in
your life.

3. *Act lovingly.*
Those who feel guilty because they can't always love are
not alone. That's the price of being human. Emotions often
wander from our nobler inclinations.

We may not always feel love, but there is never a time
when we cannot act lovingly.

Although we may be disliked, treated unfairly, and
shunted aside, we can still practice love and avoid the
devastation of hate.

Love your enemies; do good to those who hate you.

If you love your enemies, then you have no enemies.
There is no person who can truly hurt you unless that
person causes you to stop loving, stop being kind, stop
being forgiving. Only by turning your loving acts into
hateful ones can you be harmed.

For what you do to others you are, in essence, doing to
yourself. Judge not! Condemn not! Forgive!

Those are nothing but thoughts and attitudes. Modern
psychology explains that the problems of nearly all relationships are caused by people not acting the way that
other people think they should act. That's judging and
condemning.

Loving is thinking and doing. It starts out as an attitude and ends up as an emotion. Many try to reverse this.
They wait around for the emotion, expecting their minds to
be filled with exotic thoughts. It seldom happens.

Love is a feeling. It is caring, giving, and doing. The
doing is one way of getting the feeling. Expand and deepen
the feeling through acts of love. They can be simple things.

Say "please" and "thank you." Smile. Listen. Offer
help. Give praise. Send a card. Be kind. Think of others; get
your mind off yourself. What can you do to make life a little
more pleasant for someone else—unconditionally?

Love Everything and Everybody

Love is an ability, an attitude. In fact love is little less than life itself lived in the right way, with others. It is helping rather than hurting. Anyone can love. It starts with a concern, a sensitivity to others, and it grows from there.

The capacity for loving is infinite. It expands as you live—but only if it's strengthened by thinking and doing.

The thinking comes from loving everything and everybody.

Rise above the pettiness, resentment, judgment, and prejudice. Just love.

You were born to love. You are nourished and made whole by your love. You wither and despair without it. In fact, if your body is ailing in some way, it is wise to ask yourself who it is that you are not loving.

Many serious physical ailments are induced by bitterness toward others. That bitterness can be removed by forgiving. Forgiving is merely discarding negative thoughts toward others.

Becoming more loving is the most noble of life's virtues. The wise and famed of all ages have pronounced that serving and loving others is the most sacred of all of life's purposes. It is the unfailing pathway of leaving the world a little bit better than the way you found it.

22

Be Happy!

Procrastination. Putting things off. Boredom. Going nowhere. The frustration of not getting as much out of life as
hoped for.

Those are the plagues that seem to infest the human
mood. "How can I get more done? I don't have much pep.
I get so tired all the time. Where do some people get all
that energy? How do they motivate themselves?" Those are
thoughts rummaging through a lot of minds.

The problem appears to be a natural inclination of the
human being to be a little lazy (some more than a "little").
We learn to accept, admit, and believe that about ourselves.

Yet, regardless of age, we're filled with unrestricted
energy, unused effort, and boundless potential.

So why do we feel lazy, overburdened, bored, and
weary? Why do we drift, procrastinate, do so little when
there is so much we could do?

We Train Ourselves

We make ourselves that way. We train ourselves to do
nothing rather than something. The solution to the prob-

lem is not motivating ourselves but rather purging our systems of all our demotivations.

First, it must be realized that the body is a success mechanism.

It cannot fail. It will perform exactly what it is trained to perform. The body will reflect precisely and infallibly the dictates of the mind. Those conditions are not always pleasing, but, then, neither are those thoughts being held in the mind.

So when the body seems lazy, tired, lethargic, and unresponsive, it is simply reacting to the mind's wishes. It is acting the way it has been trained to act.

Be Healthy and Happy

How can that be changed? Start with giving yourself some good reasons for wanting to change. You'll live longer. Studies undeniably reveal that the motivated, busy people keep going considerably longer than those who are floating nowhere, indifferent toward purpose and activity.

Dr. Charles William Mayo said, "I have never seen a person die from overwork, but I have seen many die from boredom."

Then there's the warmth and comfort of happiness. It is the crowning prize of the motivated.

Happiness is searching for seashells at Sanibel, trying a new recipe, walking in the rain, planting a juniper, or learning a new dance step.

It is opening all your senses to an untried experience, a new venture, or another rung up in a career. It's getting involved in something that captures you mentally, physically, and emotionally. That can be exceeding your best day's sales, carving a whistle from a willow branch, or getting the back closet slickered up.

Besides, a little hustle and bustle harvests fulfillment, satisfaction, achievement, and more than a few of life's material goodies!

Stop Training Yourself to Take It Easy

Ask people what they want in life, and they'll name all sorts of devices or circumstances that will make life easier or more comfortable for themselves. In fact the gadgets become almost a necessity in life.

A fellow realized this as he came home late one evening from work and discovered his wife had not started dinner. There had been a thunderstorm, she explained. The electricity was off.

"We have a gas stove," he reminded her.

"Yes," she said, "but the can opener is electric."

How much time did you spend last year looking for the closest parking space to wherever you were going? So much of our thoughts are devoted to trying to "take it easy," to save effort as if personal energy were scarce and limited.

It isn't! It's unlimited! Set it free! Quit holding it back!

To motivate yourself, stop demotivating yourself!

Happiness Is a Personal Quest

The hit song of 1988, "Don't Worry, Be Happy" may be the best advice for happiness since Abraham Lincoln suggested that "people are about as happy as they make up their minds to be."

Both imply that happiness is a personal responsibility. Plato, the Greek philosopher, would agree. He wrote: "The person who makes everything that leads to happiness depend upon one's self, and not upon others, has adopted the very best plan for living happily."

You cannot go to the doctor and get a prescription for happiness; nor can you buy it or even learn it from someone else. In fact, Sophie Swetchine, a French writer of the eighteenth century, commented: "The best advice on the art of being happy is about as easy to follow as advice to be well when one is sick."

That does not stop people from striving to be happy. William James, the Harvard psychologist, described the quest for happiness as the secret motive that drives everyone. That elusiveness, the lack of definition, is one of the qualities of happiness. It must be pursued to be experienced.

The Declaration of Independence does not guarantee happiness. It guarantees only the "pursuit of happiness." So we know that happiness is a do-it-yourself project. It requires a decision to find happiness.

Free your mind from worry and begin the search.

Where Do You Go from There?

In recent years the behavioral scientists' research has revealed some characteristics of the state of happiness. It is little more than what common sense would dictate. It is a comfort to know you don't have to have a doctoral degree or know the names of the stars to be happy. Your own intuition will do quite nicely.

The conclusions the researchers made are really quite simple. Exercise, eat well, and stay healthy. Married people are generally happier than single people, although there are unending exceptions. Dr. Carl Jung, the Swiss psychiatrist, declared that no person was happy who did not have a religious or spiritual orientation.

Staying busy is one requirement for happiness that has been around for years. Great Britain's famed prime minister of the 1800s, Benjamin Disraeli, noted, "Action may not always bring happiness, but there is no happiness without action."

Henry Ford confirmed the value of action in work. He said, "The object of living is work, experience, happiness. There is joy in work. All that money can do is buy us someone else's work in exchange for our own. There is no happiness except in the realization that we have accomplished something."

Just working, keeping busy, is not enough. How you

keep busy contributes to your happiness. The famed of all ages have advised that being of service to others is the elixir of happiness. Dr. Albert Schweitzer, the philosopher and missionary physician, states, "I don't know what your destiny will be, but one thing I know: the only ones among you who will be really happy are those who will have sought and found how to serve."

However, you do not have to leave all and open a hospital in Africa, as Dr. Schweitzer did, to serve. Serving can be a chain of small services that originate somewhere around the heart. That can be done with a family, at work, or in daily contact with others. It means giving of yourself.

Charles Burr put it this way: "Getters generally don't get happiness; givers get it. You simply give to others a bit of yourself—a thoughtful act, a helpful idea, a word of appreciation, a lift over a rough spot, a sense of understanding, a timely suggestion; you take something out of your mind, garnished in kindness out of your heart, and put it into another person's mind and heart."

The world's great religions have always proclaimed the path to happiness in just one word. *Love*. Love yourself. Love others. Happiness revolves around your relationship with others.

Being happy is little more than an understanding and application of the fundamental truths of life. It cannot be found in things or money or fast living. It is taking the time to discover all that you have within you. Share some with others. Observe the basic lessons of life originating from the hearts and minds of civilization over the ages.

A Formula for Happiness

Write down the names of ten people you know best outside your family.

After each name, write either *H* (for happy) or *N* (for unhappy).

Then go down the list again, writing *S* (for selfish) or *U* (for unselfish) after each name.

Did your rating reveal a style of conduct for being happy?

Out of two thousand people graded by this system, only seventy-eight were designated as being happy/selfish. Apparently those people who are devoted to bringing happiness only to themselves rarely succeed. The survey indicated that the large majority of happy people are those who help others become happy.

It has been said many ways through the ages, hasn't it? Give freely to others what you cherish for yourself.

Admittedly there are people who are motivated out of sheer selfishness. And many are successful. But are they happy? Rarely, for they are driven by an urge that is never content—selfishness.

In contrast, consider the person motivated by the unselfish compulsion to share, serve, and help others. Every day is filled with moments of deep satisfaction as the needs of others are met. That is the person who can look within his or her own heart and like what is found there. Without that attribute, there can be no happiness.

Say Yes to Happiness

Why not double your happiness? Why not double your moments of joy?

That may not be as impossible as it seems. Indeed it may be as simple as saying yes rather than no. Say yes rather than no to all the possibilities of life.

As an adult you face each day from one or two positions. You defend or you learn. You protect or you grow.

Think about that. Either you are protecting and defending yourself, or you are learning and growing. You can't do both. If you're protecting and defending the way you're working, for instance, it's difficult to learn and grow. You don't change by rigidly protecting and defending who you are and what you're doing.

To learn and grow, decide that you're willing to

change. Then open your mind. You need not discard your old beliefs and habits. Just set them aside for a moment. Say yes to life.

Open Your Mind

Be willing to listen to others, especially those who have contrasting ideas to yours. In fact, be more than willing. Seek out new ideas and different paths to new goals. Open the channels of your thoughts so that life can flow through you unobstructed. Learn to look at every situation in life as a possibility rather than as a problem or an obstacle.

Say yes to your wonder and magnificence. Stop thinking that incredible success belongs only to others. You are ready right now. And the world is for you—not against you. Don't fall into the trap of letting life happen while you're making other plans.

Hold these thoughts in your consciousness: Life is not what is happening someday. The only life that you can know is today, this hour, this minute. Say yes to the moment! This day can be twice as joyous as yesterday if you believe it. You choose the results of your life by choosing your thoughts.

Say yes to those inner urges, the sleeping dreams and the timid hopes. Your instincts are crying out desperately for you to say yes to the greatness and the limitless potential within you.

You don't become important by looking for problems or by making others feel unimportant. Nor do you do it by defending and protecting the way you are or the rituals and habits of your life. Change, admittedly, can be risky. It means leaving where you are and not coming back, stepping out of the comfort zone and becoming uncomfortable. That requires mental and physical stamina, courage, and even some distress. It's easier to say no to that than yes. But those *no*s are ways of simply repeating what the past has been. Saying yes opens up all sorts of possibilities.

Don't decide to say yes for a day or two and expect your life to change. Make it a way of life.

You don't want to be like the fellow on the opening day of the fishing season. He rolled out of bed, picked up a fishing rod that had some strange plug attached, and went out on the dock. With the first cast he caught a twenty-six-inch fish. He cast again and caught another fish, a little smaller. He caught another on his third cast, a pretty big one. On his fourth cast, nothing.

He threw the rod down and went back inside, muttering to himself, "To heck with it! They just ain't biting!"

Keep throwing out those *yes*es and you'll catch some whoppers!

You will also catch that elusive quality that is the object of all life—happiness!